TRAVELING BY GONDOLA, ENJOYING CREAMY *RISI E BISI* FOR LUNCH, SPLASH-ING THROUGH STREETS THAT FLOOD WHEN THE TIDE IS HIGH—THIS IS EVERYDAY LIFE FOR SKYE McALPINE. She has lived in Venice for most of her life, moving there from London when she was six years old, and she's learned from years of sharing meals with family and neighbors how to cook the Venetian way. With *A Table in Venice* you can discover how to cook traditional dishes as well as Skye's take on classics, including Bigoli with Creamy Walnut Sauce, Scallops on the Shell with Pistachio Gratin, Grilled Radicchio with Pome-granate, and Chocolate and Amaretto Custard. The 100 irresistible recipes, stunning photography, and beautiful storytelling will bring this lovely city to life in your very own home.

A TABLE IN VENICE

SKYE McALPINE

A TABLE IN VENICE

RECIPES FROM MY HOME

CLARKSON POTTER/PUBLISHERS
New York

Library of Congress Cataloging-in-
Publication Data

Names: McAlpine, Skye, author.
Title: A table in Venice: recipes from my
home / Skye McAlpine.
Description: First edition. | New York :
Clarkson Potter/Publishers, [2018] |
Includes index.
Identifiers: LCCN 2017028055 (print) |
LCCN 2017033445 (ebook) | ISBN
9781524760304 (ebook) | ISBN
9781524760298 (hardcover).
Subjects: LCSH: Cooking, Italian. |
LCGFT: Cookbooks.
Classification: LCC TX723 (ebook) |
LCC TX723 .M39 2018 (print) | DDC
641.5945--dc23.
LC record available at https://lccn.loc.
gov/2017028055.

ISBN 978-1-5247-6029-8

Ebook ISBN 978-1-5247-6030-4

Printed in China

Book and cover design by Marysarah Quinn
Photographs by Skye McAlpine

10 9 8 7 6 5 4 3 2 1

FIRST EDITION

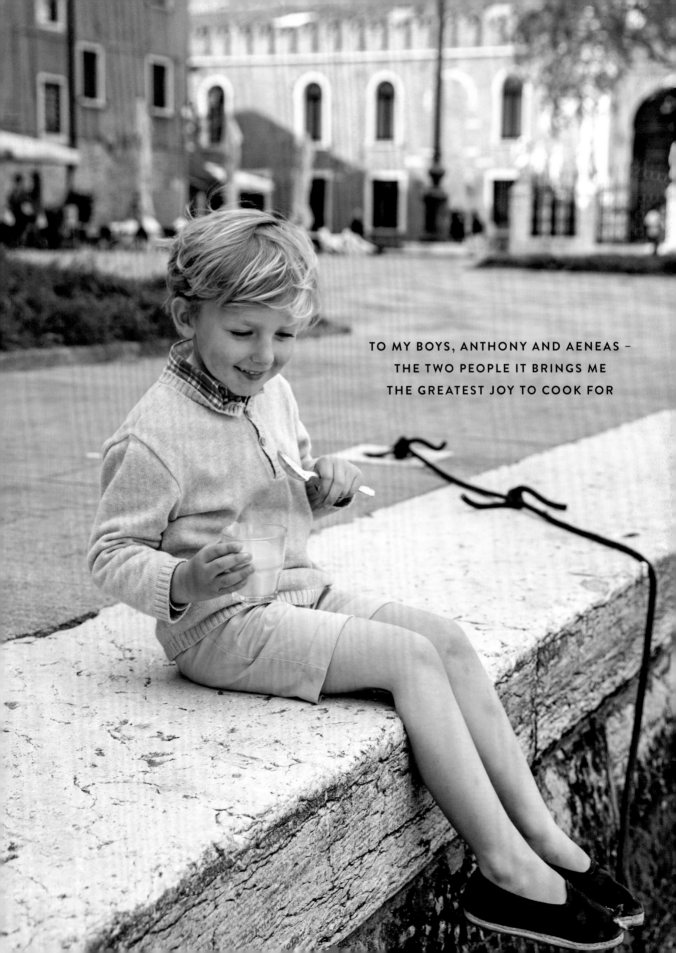

TO MY BOYS, ANTHONY AND AENEAS –
THE TWO PEOPLE IT BRINGS ME
THE GREATEST JOY TO COOK FOR

INTRODUCTION 9

MY VENETIAN PANTRY 17

IL CAFÉ 23
SWEET BREAKFAST RECIPES

IL MERCATO 67
VEGETABLE RECIPES FROM THE RIALTO MARKET

A TAVOLA 115
CLASSIC LUNCH RECIPES

LO SPRITZ 168
RECIPES FOR A VENETIAN APERITIVO

LA LAGUNA 201
FISH AND GAME FROM THE VENETIAN LAGOON

LA PASTICCERIA 241
DESSERTS AND SWEET TREATS

ACKNOWLEDGMENTS 280

INDEX 282

CONTENTS

INTRODUCTION

IN A QUIET CORNER OF VENICE, far off the beaten track and away from the crowds that cluster around the famous Piazza San Marco, stands a little house. Its walls are a dirty and crumbling pink plaster. Its windows, hidden behind watermelon-green shutters, look out over a sleepy canal. Were you wandering past, you most likely would not look at it twice, too beguiled by the riches and beauty the streets of Venice have to offer all around you. Were you wandering past, you might even be lost—few visitors bother coming to this unpretentious part of town by intention. But were you to pause for a moment, standing just outside the green door, in the *campo* where the cherry tree grows; were you to stop and look, what you would see is my home. The house where I grew up, where my husband and I celebrated our wedding, where my son took his first steps, and where I learned to cook.

The story of how the little pink house on a Venetian backwater came to be my home is a serendipitous one. Unlike almost everyone else in my neighborhood, I wasn't born in Venice, nor is my family from there: we moved to the city when I was tiny and before I can really remember living anywhere else. I have no recollection of my first night in the attic bedroom at the top of our house, for example, or of seeing the city for the first time from the water. Most distinctly, I remember my mother telling me that we were to move there for a year—and my asking if this meant that I wouldn't have to go to school. I was six.

I did go to school, of course; and we stayed longer than a year. We've never really left.

When we first arrived, I spoke not a word of Italian beyond *ciao* and *gelato*. I went to the local Italian school, a charming old convent with vaulted ceilings and the prettiest of courtyards. My teacher was a petite nun with a kindly, creased face who wore an immaculately starched white wimple. We called her *Madre Adolfa* and, with all the patience in the world, she taught me Italian. She spoke no English. I remember her running water from a rusty tap into her hands, jabbing her wet finger at me, and crying "*goccia, goccia!*" the Italian word for "drop of water."

For a long time, I thought that *goccia* meant "finger." I soon learned to speak Italian, though with a heavy Venetian accent and a fair few words of dialect mixed in. And with time, the strangeness of living in a city with no cars, traveling everywhere by boat, and splashing through the streets flooded with water when the tide comes in high became my every day, though for me it has never lost its charm. As is often the way when you come from one place and live in another, I feel no identifiable nationality: I am neither wholly English nor wholly Italian, but I am much of both. Venice, really, has always been home; and with time, I have come to think of myself as Venetian, if only by adoption.

As is the way for so many of us who love to eat, my happiest childhood memories are centered on food. And as I've grown older, little has changed for me on that front. I remain the kind of greedy person who remembers and feels life through what she ate and how it was cooked: veal scallops, rolled in crisp bread crumbs and cooked *alla milanese*, on our wedding night; panettone filled with pistachio cream for pudding the Christmas before last; *bollito misto* with a very sharp *salsa verde* on the day my husband proposed; and cold tongue with heaps of Dijon mustard followed by a molten hot chocolate soufflé the night before our son, Aeneas, was born.

I live by the belief that food is so much more than necessity. It is memories and feelings; it's both a reflection of and a catalyst for your mood; it is a profound way to connect with those we are privileged enough to share a meal with.

As I was growing up, we cooked often at home. My parents loved few things in life more than to gather around a dining table for lunch and linger there until long past the sun's setting. Meals were usually chaotic: shared plates, hastily tossed together; flowers, cut higgledy-piggledy from the garden and plonked casually on the table. Sometimes lunch for six, though just as often for twelve or even twenty. The more the merrier—the hum of excitable conversation playing out to a satisfying chorus of knives and forks scraping on plates, and strains of Verdi opera blaring from the tinny stereo in the kitchen. To me the chaos was magic. My memories are fully of warmth, generosity, and, above all, fun. Our life played out around the dining table, and it was made richer by the food we ate and by the cast of characters who joined us there. Somewhere along the way, I learned both to cook and to love to cook.

VENICE'S BEST-KEPT SECRET

If you know Italy well, you will know that each corner of the country, each region, boasts its own distinct cuisine, just as it speaks its own local dialect and lives by an indefatigable sense of regional pride. It is perhaps not so surprising, when you think that Italy only became Italy, as such, in 1861. Before then, what we now think of as one country was simply a collection of independent principalities and city-states that shared little more than geography.

All of this is by way of some explanation of the fact that when you talk to a Sicilian about Italian food, they will regale you with tales of pizza and cannoli, and when you talk to a Roman, you will hear of deep-fried artichokes and *cacio e pepe*. An Italian's view on what makes for "real Italian" food still now is determined by where he or she is from, just as their view on how tomato sauce should be prepared is determined by how his or her own mother cooks it. The one constant across the country: the beautiful simplicity and infectious passion with which all Italians cook and eat.

Venice only became part of Italy in 1866, having passed from the rule of Napoleon to the Austrians in 1797. Before that, through the Middle Ages and the Renaissance, it dominated the Mediterranean as an independent republic, as *La Serenissima*. Over the course of its rich history, the city welcomed crusaders, merchants, pilgrims, artists, revelers, romantics, travelers, traders from the East and West alike. They have all left a little of themselves behind, and together they have contributed to building an extraordinary city that is quite like no other. These many and varied influences are reflected in Venice's food, just as they are in its crumbling walls and famed frescoes.

Venetian food—and by that I mean the food eaten by Venetians—remains perhaps Italy's best-kept secret. It is certainly a closely guarded one. Hundreds of thousands of visitors pass through the city each month, and they eat at *trattorie* that cater to a transient trade and leave having eaten in Venice, but not having eaten well. It is the food cooked in homes and made with local ingredients, the recipes passed down through generations, that Venetians guard ferociously and exclusively for their own gratification. That is Venetian food; that is what I love and that is what I write about here.

This cuisine is romantic and it is exotic. It dabbles in spices and delightfully foreign flavors. It's pine nuts and raisins, bay leaves and sweet vinegar, heady saffron and creamy mascarpone. *Zabaione* custard, for which you whip Prosecco, eggs, and sugar into a frenzy as light as air, and then eat it by the spoonful; buttery *risotto* made with garden peas so sweet and tender you would be forgiven for mistaking the dish for a pudding. For me, it is the food of my childhood, laden with nostalgia and synonymous with comfort.

The process of writing this book has been a great joy for me for many reasons, not least because it has given me the excuse (if, in fact, an excuse was needed) to unearth and cook from as many old Venetian cookbooks as I could lay my hands on. Some were books I remember my mother cooking from and that have sat collecting dust on our bookshelves or in boxes in our attic for years; others, unassuming secondhand books largely written in dialect, with no pictures to recommend them but devoted to topics as niche as the asparagus in the Veneto region, Jewish food culture in Venice, or the traditional foods of the patron saint days, all brimming with delightful recipes. The process has taken me on a journey during which I found myself revisiting beautiful recipes that have long since fallen out of fashion and cooking for the first time ancient dishes I remember hearing about as a child, but had never tasted before.

Those recipes I found myself cooking again and again are the ones that made their way into this book.

HOW I COOK

I am not a chef, nor do I have any formal training. I have little to recommend me in the kitchen beyond my greed, curiosity, and the fact that the kitchen is where I have always found myself to be happiest. Growing up, I would watch my mother for hours as she transformed flour, butter, and eggs into cake, pasta, and pastry. I learned how to roll gnocchi from my friend Ornella; and from her mother, Maria, how to mix a cup of cooking water into any pasta sauce, so it tastes impossibly creamy even when made without any cream. I learned how to make really good, buttery cookies from my great-aunt, and how to knead pizza dough from our local *pizzaiolo*, Paolo.

Everything I know about cooking comes from a lifetime spent watching what others do, then replicating it in my own kitchen. I've learned from trial and error; from too much time spent exploring the market, chatting with market vendors; and from too many afternoons spent leafing through cookbooks. I am driven by the belief that no matter how glamorous the restaurant or how fancy its food, eating out could never be quite as big a treat as eating in, and so that is what I write about: simple, beautiful home cooking.

I make no lofty claims of compiling a definitive, or even a compre-hensive, catalogue of "authentic" Venetian food, nor would I want to. All I have to offer is an honest account of how I live and love the city, and what it means to me. You will find some traditional Venetian dishes missing in this book: *baccalà alla Veneziana*, for example, for which you soak salt cod in water for days, then poach it in milk and whip it up with olive oil. I love to eat *baccalà*, but I do so when I go to a restaurant for dinner. I would never think to cook it at home, and so I found its recipe had no legitimate place here.

For lack of a better word, you might call this collection of recipes my "take" on Venetian cuisine. Collected together, these are the dishes I cook time and time again at home, those which mean the most to me and which have provided me with the greatest joy over the years. Together they make up how I cook. Simple, fresh, colorful—always plentiful—Venetian, if only by adoption.

MY VENETIAN PANTRY

BEYOND THE STAPLES THAT MOST OF us tend to have in our fridge and cupboard—butter, sugar, milk, and so forth—here is a list of ingredients I cook with time and time again, and that you will find cropping up, like a recurring chorus, in many of the recipes in this book. Most are widely available in well-stocked supermarkets or Italian delicatessens. Where the ingredients might be thought of as specialist, I have also recommended good substitutes.

AMARETTO BISCUITS

Amaretti are sweet, macaroon-like light cookies made with sugar, egg whites, and crushed almonds or apricot kernels. There are two different kinds of amaretti. One is the soft and chewy variety, which are fancier and come individually wrapped in beautiful pastel-colored papers; these are best eaten as is and make a lovely accompaniment to coffee after dinner. The other variety are smaller, deeper in color, and crisp on the outside: these are the ones I use often in cooking, be it crumbled over chocolate (page 254), with custard or zabaione (page 62), or paired with pumpkin (page 144). It's good to have a box of them on hand because they have an uncanny way of becoming useful.

ANCHOVIES

When I refer to anchovies, I am talking about the ones that have been filleted, salt-cured, and then stored in olive oil. They come in small jars or cans, and they keep in your cupboard forever. Not all anchovies, however, are created equal, so I tend to invest in the more expensive brands. They are the kind of ingredient I add to many things to lend a little something extra to the dish; the Peperonata on page 98 is perhaps my favorite example.

CANDIED PEEL

Candied peel is a recurring theme in the canon of Italian desserts, and Venetian sweets are no exception.

There is something deliciously extravagant about citrus fruits laden with sugar; they add a lovely depth to creamy puddings, as well as to pastries and breads. I buy candied peel from the spice shop in Venice: it comes in thick strips, with a sugar crusting that glistens seductively, and it tastes both pungent and sweet. Most Italian delicatessens, dotted around the world, sell this kind of rich candied peel. It's worth stocking up on when you have the chance, as it keeps well and always comes in handy. You can, of course, buy peel from the supermarket: it tends to come ready chopped and in small tubs. This, I find, does well as a substitute in baking, but somehow doesn't quite compare to the "special stuff."

CHEESE

Cheese is one of the largest Italian food exports, and wherever in the world you are, you will most likely find some excellent Italian cheeses at the local supermarkets or at Italian delicatessens. The cheeses I cook with most regularly are not particular to the Veneto region but, rather, are constants through Italian cooking and are particular favorites of mine.

I keep a pot of grated **Parmesan**—or **grana,** as we call it in Venice—in my fridge. It is placed at the center of the table for every meal, so we can all spoon it greedily over our pasta, soup, risotto, what have you. Whole chunks of Parmesan, wrapped in paper and stored in the fridge, will keep well for several weeks; once grated, however, the cheese loses its flavor and goes stale within days. On occasion, when I'm pressed for time, I have been known to buy the cheese that comes ready grated and sealed in plastic bags, though I have always been disappointed: it never tastes as good.

I also like to keep fresh **mozzarella** on hand to eat with a little oil, salt, and perhaps a few sprigs of mint or basil; or to use in cooking. Always buy good-quality mozzarella, which should come shaped like a creamy white tennis ball and be swimming in a tub

BIGOLI IN SALSA

WHEN I OPEN MY FRIDGE to find nothing that resembles supper, I make *bigoli in salsa*: a pasta with a heavenly, creamy sauce of onion and anchovies. Peel and roughly slice a large white onion, toss it in a pan with 3 to 4 tablespoons of olive oil, and cook gently until it softens and turns translucent, 8 to 10 minutes. Toss in 8 anchovy fillets and simmer gently until the sauce turns into a soft mush, roughly 5 minutes. Cook the pasta per the instructions on the package. Stir 1 cup of the cooking water into the sauce and toss in the pasta. I can't tell you how good this is.

of milky water. Buffalo mozzarella, which I prefer, is lighter and has a more distinctive flavor than the cow's milk variety.

In recipes that call for melted cheese, I tend to favor **Taleggio**—a lovely semisoft cheese with a thick rind that's made in the Alpine valley—for both its heavenly texture and its strong flavor. You can substitute with Edam, Gouda, or Gruyère, if need be.

Though technically a cheese, **mascarpone,** rich and creamy, tastes closer to something like a delicate variation on clotted cream. I find I cook with it often and in so many different ways, both sweet and savory. At La Casa del Parmigiano, the cheese shop just by the Rialto, they sell it by weight and spoon it out from a large tub onto sheets of paper, then carefully wrap it into little packages; but in most supermarkets, you can buy mascarpone prepackaged in tubs. I always like to have mascarpone on hand; wonderfully versatile, I use it for anything from mixing into steaming hot pasta with a little Parmesan as a sauce, to whipping it up into a buttercream of sorts with a little confectioners' sugar. Or I might serve dollops of it with fresh strawberries, fruit crumble, poached or stewed fruit, or spooned into a cup with a drizzle of chocolate sauce and a few crumbled amaretti biscuits for dessert.

Finally, **ricotta** is light and spreadable, and pairs beautifully with most things, especially fresh fruit. Not utterly unlike cream cheese, it has a grainier texture. Ricotta is available in most supermarkets these days. Though, as a side note, you could make your own: slowly bring 8 cups of whole milk to a boil in a heavy-bottomed pan over medium heat (to stop it from scorching), stirring occasionally; reduce the heat to a low simmer and add ⅓ cup fresh lemon juice, stirring constantly until the mixture curdles, about 2 minutes. Let the mixture sit for 10 minutes, then pour into a lined strainer or cheesecloth and let drain for about 30 minutes. Refrigerate until you are ready to eat. The cheese will keep for up to two days.

CHOCOLATE

The difference between good- and not-good-quality chocolate cannot be overestimated. Always buy the best you can afford and get your hands on, and make sure you are using dark chocolate with a high cocoa percentage (generally 70% or 85%) when baking for grown-ups and children alike—never use milk chocolate. You will thank me for it. Good-quality dark chocolate is infinitely richer and deeper in flavor than its milk counterpart.

FLOUR

If you enjoy baking or eating freshly baked goods (and in my experience, the two tend to go hand in hand), you should have a pantry that is well stocked with flour. I store mine in large glass jars and on open shelves, so that I can easily see when and on what I'm running low. I clearly label the jars with stickers underneath, so that I can see what is what. Different kinds of flour suit different moods and dishes. **All-purpose flour** is best for making batter, for dusting pork or veal chops before you pan-fry them, for making cookies, for thickening sauces and custards, and the like. **Self-rising flour,** which has baking powder already incorporated in it, is ideal for cakes when you want a nice rise. (If you need to, you can mix up your own self-rising flour by combining 1 cup of all-purpose flour with 1½ teaspoons baking powder and ¼ teaspoon fine salt.) **Bread flour** has a higher gluten content, which when activated with yeast, allows more air to be incorporated and trapped in the dough, for a higher rising bread.

Italian flours are graded "1," "0," and "00," depending on the fineness of the grind; **Italian-type "00" flour** is more refined and finer than all-purpose flour. While the one can be substituted for the other in most instances, when baking a sponge cake, for example, type "00" will give you a cake with a lighter, fluffier crumb. Type "00" is

also most widely used for making fresh pasta and pizza dough.

HERBS

Fresh herbs, fragrant and roughly torn, scattered over a dish in a haphazard manner—that is how I cook. In our garden in Venice, we keep herbs in pots: **basil, rosemary, thyme, parsley, lemon verbena,** and **sage.** I grew up in the habit of running out into the garden to pick rosemary when we needed it for the potatoes, or mint (or lemon verbena) to stew briefly in a pot of boiling water to make fresh tea. You can, of course, buy herbs from the supermarket in little plastic bags, and these are fine—they're also quite expensive and have an uncanny way of wilting within hours of opening the packet. Some markets and farmers' markets sell fresh herbs in bunches, and these keep longer. Far more rewarding and convenient is to grow your own herbs in pots—be it in your garden, on a windowsill, or near the kitchen sink if it's a sunny spot. For the lazy and slightly chaotic cook, like me, it is essential.

OLIVE OIL

Olive oil is at the heart of Italian cooking. Just as there are countless varieties of grapes and wines, so there are many kinds of olives and olive oil. And although convention (and some degree of snobbery) would suggest that there are "good" and "bad" bottles, it really boils down to a matter of what you like. Let your taste buds be your guide. Unlike wine, however, bear in mind that olive oil doesn't improve with age: it is perishable and, ideally, never better than when enjoyed a few weeks after it is made. Olives are stone fruits, like cherries and peaches, so you can think of extra-virgin olive oil (made by pressing the olives without adding any heat) much like fresh juice. Buy smaller bottles and refresh your stores regularly. Many cook with one common kind of olive oil, and then reserve a fancier variety for eating raw—with salads, bread, and so forth. I take the easy route of having just one bottle, usually Filippo Berio, which I keep on our kitchen counter and use liberally with everything.

PASTA

Our kitchen shelves are always well stocked with dried pasta: plenty of it and many different kinds. This means that, at a moment's notice, I can toss together a plate of spaghetti, drizzle with oil, sprinkle with a few red pepper flakes, add a little garlic, and have ourselves a very fine *spaghetti aglio, olio, e peperoncino* for dinner. While pasta is pasta, its shape will vary the texture to such a point that you could almost swear it tastes different. Pairing of pasta with sauces is a fine art. As a rule of thumb: the thinner cut pastas—spaghetti, linguine, and the like—are best suited to lighter sauces, cream based, or fresh seafood; the thicker cut pastas—tagliatelle, pappardelle, fettuccine, or malfatti—work very nicely with richer, meatier sauces. Penne, rigatoni, and conchiglioni, which have a way of filling up nicely with sauce, are best for rich baked pasta dishes; while tiny maccheroni and the like are ideally suited to add to broths and soups. Dried pasta keeps well, in either a sealed packet or a jar. I always make a point of buying good-quality pasta, because the difference in taste is distinctly noticeable: make sure the pasta is made from durum wheat semolina only (no other preservatives or additives) and that it is a uniform, rich yellow color.

PINE NUTS

Pine nuts, often paired with sweet raisins, appear frequently in traditional Venetian cooking, and so I cook with them often. They have an uncanny way≈of adding depth, texture, and flavor to even the simplest of dishes. They are the seeds embedded in pine cones, and as they are difficult to harvest, consequently they are also quite expensive to buy. Buy good Italian pine nuts, if you can find them (the majority of pine nuts for sale today are imported from China); they are wonderfully creamy and as much of a delight in sweet cakes as they are lightly toasted, sprinkled over a plate of greens, or served with fish (page 220).

POLENTA

Polenta is cornmeal that, when cooked with bubbling salted water and a little butter, morphs into the fluffy, creamy comfort food of Northern Italy. You can eat polenta many ways: cook it so that it's runny and creamy, then perhaps serve it with shrimp and a drizzle of oil (see page 219), or top with rich meatballs laden with thick tomato sauce (see page 166). Or, let the polenta cool and firm up, then grill it briefly on a hot griddle so that it turns deliciously crisp on the outside. You can buy polenta called *biancoperla*, which means "whiter than white," and it's wonderfully delicate in flavor—heaven when paired with seafood. Or, polenta can be the color of yellow corn, thick and rougher in taste and texture—the kind of thing you imagine eating with stews and grilled meats. If you are pressed for time, you can buy instant polenta, which is quicker cooking and certainly easy to make, though it doesn't have quite the same flavor as the longer cooking variety. Polenta is not so much about speed as it is the comforting ritual of simple, repetitive cooking: it is food for cold days, when watching a pot of it bubble gently and pausing from time to time to give it a stir is a pleasure rather than an obligation.

PROSECCO

The town of Prosecco is not far from Venice. And Glera grapes, formerly known as Prosecco grapes, are widely harvested in the Veneto region to make a light and bubbly wine. It's rather like Champagne, though somewhat less fancy and a fraction of the price. Prosecco is what you use to mix a Bellini (page 198) or a Spritz (page 197). You will find it offered, by the carafe, at any good *trattoria* in Venice; on occasion you might use it in cooking—to make zabaione, for example (page 109). I always keep a couple of bottles in the fridge.

PUFF PASTRY (PREPARED FROZEN OR REFRIGERATED)

In no way particular to the Venetian way of cooking, or to Italian cuisine either for that matter, prepared puff pastry is an ingredient I use so often and with such exceptional results when cooking at home that I couldn't leave it off this list of pantry essentials. It is almost impossible to tell the difference between a good-quality packaged puff pastry and the homemade variety, so use the commercial type with impunity and don't look back. My only insistence is that you take care to buy a good brand that is made with flour and butter, not any other kind of shortening.

RAISINS

Raisins are a recurring theme in Venetian food, and they are found in sweet and savory dishes alike. Because I find myself cooking with them so often, I like to make sure I have a jar on hand to toss some into a cake, or to mix with softly cooked onion to make *in saor* sauce (see page 97). Generally, raisins can be a little dry, so I like to soak them in a splash of alcohol before adding them to the dish; they become deliciously plump.

RICE

I rarely cook rice except to make risotto—but I cook risotto often, as it is one of my favorite things to eat. Risotto should be almost like pudding, but never mushy. I use *arborio* rice, which when cooked in a mixture of stock and white wine makes a wonderfully creamy risotto, yet each grain of rice still holds its distinct shape and a chewy bite at its core. Some prefer *carnaroli* rice, which has a longer grain and tends to take a little longer to cook, but also holds its shape better. For Risi e Bisi (page 157), I prefer *vialone nano*, which has small grains that are well suited to a more soupy risotto.

SAFFRON

While it's not local to Venice, much Venetian food is laced with the heady aroma and golden hues of saffron. The story of how this precious spice reached Venice after traveling far and wide would fill the pages of a hefty book. I give saffron its own mention here because I use it so often in my cooking. Even today, saffron is more expensive per gram than gold—the strands (stigmas) gathered from thousands upon thousands of crocus flowers, which are harvested by hand and then dried. Only a pinch of saffron is enough to turn a dish into something at once sumptuous and warm. In Venice, we use saffron mostly with fish and seafood, in risottos, and in creamy pasta sauces. Less conventional but with no less exquisite results, I add saffron to mayonnaise, zabaione, panna cotta, whipped cream, poached fruit and syrups, and—a particular favorite of mine—soft scrambled eggs.

In Italy, saffron is most widely available in powdered form: it comes in tiny paper sachets with a standard weight of 0.125g. One sachet is usually enough to infuse a risotto or pasta dish with plenty of color and flavor, and can be added directly to the pan. In the United States, it is more widely sold as strands or threads. These threads give off flavor best when warmed, so you need to infuse them in a tablespoon or so of hot water for a few minutes, then strain the golden syrup and add it to your cooking. (I find that roughly ½ teaspoon of saffron threads equates to a sachet of powdered saffron, and

I have provided indications in the recipes accordingly.) Alternatively, you can add a pinch of salt to the saffron threads and use a pestle and mortar to grind them into a fine powder that you can add, as is, to your cooking.

SALT

Venice was built with salt; perhaps not literally, but there was a time, as long ago as the twelfth century, when Venice ran a monopoly in the salt trade that extended across the Adriatic and the Mediterranean. Many a fancy palazzo we see today was built with profits from the salt trade. It was called "white gold," a luxury and precious commodity in a world in which there were few other ways to preserve food. These days, of course, salt is neither particularly fancy nor expensive, but it holds prominence in determining the difference between a bland and an exquisite meal. I was told once that you should salt food as much as it can take before it begins to taste too salty, and that is largely how I cook. I keep three kinds of salt in our kitchen. One is **rock salt,** which I mostly use for salting pasta water and occasionally also for salt-baking fish (see page 229). Another is **table salt,** which I might add to dishes as I cook them—to doughs, to batters, even to pasta sauce or to risotto. And the third is the **salt flakes,** Maldon salt or kosher salt, which I use for dressing food just before serving.

SPICES

If you wander the streets of Venice today you will find the city to be old and faded, and therein, of course, lies much of its charm. Yet once upon a time, Venice was a bustling metropolis, a far-reaching power built mostly on the trade of spices. The gateway between the East and the West, the city's rich and checkered past is reflected in the way we still cook there today, in the unique pairing of the fresh flavors of Italian cooking with deliciously exotic spices: delicate sole

fillets served with saffron (see page 226), for example; cardamom-laced puddings (see page 30); and fresh ginger dipped in sugar.

When you open a jar of spice, it should smell so strongly of the ingredient that it transports you to another world. If the scent seems pale, most likely it will taste pale and it is best to start again; for that very reason, I take care to buy spices in the smallest quantities and to top up my stores regularly. My essentials are **bay leaves, fennel seeds, aniseed, cloves, cinnamon, nutmeg, ground ginger, red pepper flakes, paprika, cumin,** and some spice mixes like **pumpkin pie spice.**

STOCKS OR BROTHS

Stock, or a strongly flavored broth, is a recurring theme in many a recipe, from risotto to soups, to pot roasts when you are cooking gamier, tougher meat (page 238). The difference between a good stock and a poor-quality stock is so dramatic that I hesitate to call them both by the same name. Always use the best stock you can get your hands on. In an ideal world, you would make your own, at home. **Vegetable broth** is simple to make, and you can store it in the fridge in an airtight container for up to a week, or in the freezer for up to three months: add a mix of roughly chopped onions, celery stalks, carrots, fennel, leeks, fresh thyme, bay leaves, and parsley to a large casserole dish; cover with enough water so that you can easily stir them, set over medium-high heat, and bring to a boil. Leave to bubble away on medium-high heat for an hour, until the water is nicely infused with the flavor of the vegetables. Remove the vegetables with a slotted spoon, then pass the broth through a strainer before you use it.

A **chicken** or **meat stock** is a little more labor intensive, though barely; see page 128 for a recipe. If you are using commercial stock, preferably buy the kind in pouches because it is relatively freshly made.

IL CAFÉ

SWEET BREAKFAST
RECIPES

BREAKFAST IN VENICE ALMOST DOESN'T SEEM like breakfast at all. Something sweet—warm pastries, polenta cookies laced with plump raisins, perhaps a slice of soft cake covered in confectioners' sugar or peppered with minced cooked apple—washed down with a cup of milky coffee. It's frivolous and extravagant, and while it unabashedly makes no promise of healthfulness, it is an irresistibly fun way to start the day.

My favorite breakfast is what we in Venice call *brioche*. These are pastries that, confusingly, bear little resemblance to the French brioche and are rather more like croissants made with a dough that is not so flaky and is rather softer and sweeter. And most important, when you break a brioche open, at its center is a sweet filling—apricot jam, most often. Early mornings in Venice, for me, are the scent of freshly baking brioche: in those first hours of the day, it wafts through the streets, as the cafés open their doors readying themselves for the morning breakfast rush and their bakers churn out sweet goods from the ovens.

The coffee shops are busiest at this time. Most Venetians eat breakfast on the go, standing at the bar of a favorite café, on their way to work, school, the market—wherever the business of the day might be taking them. And while to eat your meal standing up might seem to defy every rule of civilized behavior, there is something convivial about this custom. With your morning coffee and pastry at the bar comes an exchange of niceties—a catch-up on the weather, on the tides, on the local gossip—with the barista who daily makes your coffee, but also with your neighbors breakfasting alongside you and jostling for a spot to rest their coffee cup (always a proper china cup) at the bar.

This is how I grew up eating breakfast. And still now, most days, we make a point as a family of eating breakfast at the café. Most days we go to the tiny, bustling, family-run spot just round the corner from our house, the one we have affectionately come to call "the Orange Café." I think we call it that because once upon a time there were a few orange-colored tables in the back room, and while they might have long since been removed, the name has stuck, enshrined in our family lore.

It is perhaps the greatest irony that breakfast is the meal I most rarely cook, yet these recipes—brioche, pastries, sweet biscuits, cakes, and so forth—are the ones I take the greatest pleasure in making. And so I make them for us to eat at tea or for dessert, just as much as I do for breakfast on those occasions when we don't eat at the bar of the Orange Café but, rather, leisurely at home around our kitchen table, with the morning papers.

APRICOT BRIOCHE

BRIOCHE ALLA MARMELLATA

MAKES 6 BRIOCHE

2¾ cups / 350g bread flour, plus
additional for dusting

¼ cup / 40g granulated sugar, plus
1 tablespoon for sprinkling

2 teaspoons / 7g instant yeast

A generous pinch of salt

1 cup (2 sticks) plus 2 tablespoons /
250g cold salted butter

½ cup / 125ml whole milk, cold

2 large eggs

2 heaping tablespoons apricot jam

AS MENTIONED IN THE CHAPTER INTRODUCTION, these are what in Venice we call *brioche*, a sort of croissant-meets-quickbread with a dollop of apricot jam in the center. The dough is rather like a French brioche, only rolled and folded several times like a croissant, which gives it a lighter, flakier texture than quickbread. The rich, buttery dough requires several risings and so you need to allow a little time to make this recipe. You might even want to leave the dough to rise overnight, and then just roll the brioche and finish them off the next morning. Bear in mind, though, that very little of that time is hands-on; mostly it's time for the dough to rest. And if you are truly pressed for time, you could make these with prepared puff pastry (see page 19). The end result won't quite have the same texture, but it will be lovely nonetheless.

I have used apricot jam, which is not just convention but also my favorite. There is no reason, though, why you shouldn't try these with strawberry, fig, or black cherry jam; or use a dollop of bitter orange marmalade, honey, or dark chocolate spread, for that matter. The possibilities are endless.

Place the flour, sugar, yeast, and salt into a food processor and pulse for a few seconds to combine. Chop the butter into pieces and add to the processor bowl. Process for a few seconds until the mixture has the consistency of coarse sand. Tip the mixture into a medium mixing bowl and set aside.

In a small bowl, whisk together the milk with one of the eggs and 3 tablespoons cold water. Make a well in the center of the flour mixture and pour the milk mixture into it. Stir with a table knife to bring the dough together into a sticky, lumpy mass. Shape the dough into a ball, set it back into the mixing bowl, cover with plastic wrap, and refrigerate for 4 hours or overnight.

Put the dough on a lightly floured work surface and roll it out into a long, thin rectangle roughly 8 by 16 inches (40–45cm by 20–25cm). Now fold the top third down and the bottom third up, as if you were folding a letter. Give it a quarter turn and roll it out into a long, thin rectangle again. Repeat the rolling, folding and rotating process a further 3 times, then leave the dough to rest on a baking tray, cover with plastic wrap, and leave in the fridge to proof for another 4 hours (or overnight). Try to move as quickly as you can with the dough, handling it as little as possible. If you find it starts to get too warm and sticky, wrap it in plastic wrap and chill in the fridge for a short while before continuing.

recipe continues

On a clean, lightly floured surface, roll out the dough to a long, thin rectangle, roughly ¼ inch thick. Cut it into six triangles, roughly 5 inches (12 to 14 cm) wide at the base and 9½ inches (24cm) long on the sides. Spoon 1 teaspoon of apricot jam onto the base of each triangle, centered and about two fingers' width away from the edges. Resist the urge to overfill here; you really just need a teaspoon or the jam will spill out of the brioche as it cooks. Fold the bottom edge of the triangle over the jam, trying to tuck it under, and roll the pastry up as tightly as you can, stretching the triangle over so its tip is tucked under the body of the croissant shape. Gently fold the tips of the pastry into the horns of a croissant, pinching the pastry where needed to seal. Repeat this with the remaining triangles.

Place the croissants on a baking sheet lined with baking parchment, cover with a clean tea towel or plastic wrap, and leave in a warm place for 1 hour until doubled in size.

Preheat the oven to 435°F.

Lightly beat the second egg with a fork, and then use a pastry brush to gently glaze the croissants with the egg. Sprinkle liberally with the tablespoon of sugar. Bake the croissants for 20 minutes, until golden. Remove from the oven and let cool slightly, then transfer to a wire rack. Let cool for at least 15 minutes before serving, or the jam will be molten. Eat while warm (sheer decadence) or at room temperature. (The brioche will keep in an airtight container for a few days.)

CARDAMOM AND CINNAMON RICE PUDDING TARTLETS

TORTINE DI RISO CON CARDAMOMO E CANNELLA

MAKES 12 TARTLETS

FOR THE PASTRY

1⅔ cups / 200g all-purpose flour

½ cup / 100g cold salted butter

¾ cup / 90g confectioners' sugar

A small pinch of salt

2 large egg yolks

FOR THE FILLING

2⅔ cups / 650ml whole milk

½ teaspoon ground cinnamon

½ teaspoon ground cardamom

½ teaspoon pumpkin pie spice

¾ cup / 150g arborio rice

⅔ cup / 130g confectioners' sugar

A pinch of salt

2 tablespoons / 25g salted butter

2 large eggs

1 large egg yolk

HALFWAY BETWEEN A CREAMY RICE PUDDING and a buttery morning pastry, these tartlets are a particular favorite of my husband's. It has become a family tradition to stop at the bar of our local café most mornings for one (or two), washed down with a milky cappuccino.

When I make tortine di riso at home, I like to add cardamom, cinnamon, and a dash of pumpkin pie spice mix to the rice as it simmers in the milk, which gives a lovely warmth to the custard filling. I make these as individual tartlets, which is how they are sold, and which makes them ideal for breakfast on the go. There is no reason, however, not to make a single large tart and serve it in slices, if you prefer.

To make the pastry, sift the flour into a large bowl and use your fingers to rub the butter into the flour. Sift in the confectioners' sugar and salt, and mix well with a wooden spoon. Add the egg yolks and bring everything together with your hands. Shape into a ball. (Alternatively, you can make the pastry in a food processor. Pour in the flour and pulse for a few seconds—to lighten it. Then add the cold butter in pieces and process until the mixture resembles coarse sand. Sift in the confectioners' sugar and salt, then process again until well combined. Remove the blade from the processor, add the egg yolks, and use your hands to bring the dough together in a ball.)

Wrap the ball of dough in plastic wrap and set in the fridge to rest for at least 30 minutes.

Meanwhile, make the filling. Combine the milk, cinnamon, cardamom, and pumpkin pie spice in a medium saucepan. Bring to a boil over medium heat, taking care not to scald the milk. Add the rice, confectioners' sugar, and salt. Lower the heat a little, and let simmer, stirring every now and then, until the milk has been completely absorbed by the rice, about 45 minutes. The mixture should resemble a thick, creamy rice pudding, and the rice should still have a little bit of a bite to it. Stir in the butter, then take the pan off the heat and set it aside to cool.

When the rice is cooled, mix in one of the eggs and the egg yolk to give it an even creamier, more custardy consistency.

Preheat the oven to 350°F.

On a clean, cool surface, roll out the pastry to roughly a ¼-inch thickness. Use a sharp knife to cut 12 pastry circles about 3 inches in diameter. Use a small round plate or saucer as a guide if you like.

Carefully press the dough circles into the cups of a muffin tin. Pierce each pastry bottom a couple of times with a fork, and then spoon the filling into the cups.

Crack the last egg into a small bowl and beat lightly with a fork. Lightly glaze the edges of the tartlets with a pastry brush.

Bake for 15 to 20 minutes, until the custard fillings are golden on top and firm in the middle (test with a toothpick) and slightly puffed up. Let cool briefly, then serve. (The tartlets will keep in an airtight container for 3 days.)

ALMOND PASTE CROISSANTS

KIEFER

MAKES 8 PASTRIES

¾ cup plus 1 tablespoon /
90g ground almonds

⅓ cup / 70g granulated sugar

½ tablespoon apricot jam

A pinch of salt

1 large egg

1 (17-ounce) package / 2 (320g)
packages prepared puff pastry,
thawed if frozen

¼ cup / 30g sliced almonds

2 tablespoons confectioners' sugar

WHEN THE AUSTRIANS OCCUPIED VENICE IN the early nineteenth century, they left behind a legacy of fine pastries, of which I can't help but feel these buttery almond brioche topped with melting confectioners' sugar are the finest example. You will see *kiefer* for sale first thing early in the morning in most cafés, and they are exquisite. As they are smaller than what we might normally think of as an almond croissant, I often manage two for breakfast, not least because they are irresistible. This recipe is almost impossibly simple to make, since I use prepared puff pastry. The most important thing to remember is to seal the pastry roll, so the filling doesn't ooze out while it cooks. Otherwise, you really can't go wrong.

Preheat the oven to 425°F. Line a baking sheet with parchment paper.

In a medium bowl, combine the almonds, granulated sugar, jam, and salt. Separate the egg and set the yolk aside. Lightly beat the egg white with a fork, then pour it into the almond mixture. Stir with a wooden spoon until you have a thick paste, rather like marzipan.

On a clean, cool surface, unfold one of the pastry sheets and cut it in half, and then cut each half into triangles that are approximately 5 inches (roughly 12 to 14cm) wide at the base and 10 inches (24cm) long. Spoon a scant teaspoon of almond paste onto the base of each triangle, centered and about two fingers from the edge of the pastry. Resist the urge to overfill; you really just need a teaspoon, or the filling will spill out as the pastry bakes. Fold the bottom edge of the triangle over the filling, trying to tuck it under, and roll the pastry up as tightly as you can. Gently fold the tips of the roll under, pinching the pastry where needed to seal. Repeat this for the remaining triangles and then repeat for the second sheet of pastry. Gently lift the pastries onto the prepared baking sheet.

Lightly beat the yolk with a fork, and then use a pastry brush to glaze the tops. Sprinkle liberally with the almonds.

Bake for 20 minutes, or until the pastry is golden all over. Remove the sheet from the oven. Sift the confectioners' sugar over them generously and while still piping hot, so that some of the sugar melts and soaks into the pastry. Let cool slightly, and then lift them off the baking sheet and onto a cooling rack. Eat while still warm or when cooled. (The pastries will keep in an airtight container for a few days.)

PEACH AND SAFFRON PASTRIES

SFOGLIATINE DI PESCA E ZAFFERANO

MAKES 4 PASTRIES

3 tablespoons / 60g peach jam

Scant teaspoon saffron threads (optional)

4 to 5 small peaches

1 sheet (½ a 17-ounce package) / 1 (320g) package prepared puff pastry, thawed if frozen

3 tablespoons / 45ml heavy cream

1 large egg

THESE ARE ABSOLUTELY A TREAT. The recipe is neither traditional nor canonical, but an invention of mine inspired by the buttery apple pastries at our local café that are a particular favorite with every member of our family. They really do taste their best when freshly baked and still warm from the oven, and since they call for admittedly (very) little forethought and some time, I reserve making them for weekends, when mornings tend to get off to a slower start. I think they do just as well as dessert, too, served with a pitcher of cream on the side to drizzle over. The pinch of saffron is entirely optional, though to my mind peach and saffron is a match made in heaven.

Preheat the oven to 350°F. Line a baking sheet with parchment paper.

Spoon the jam into a small saucepan (if the jam is very chunky, you can press it through a sieve first, if you want a smoother texture), add the saffron, and set over low heat until it begins to bubble. Remove the pan from the heat and let cool.

Cut the peaches in half, discard the stones, then finely slice the fruit into half-moon slivers. These can be as chunky or as fine as you like.

Unfold and lay the puff pastry sheet on a clean, cool surface and use a sharp knife to cut it into 4 strips equal in size. Gently place the pastry on the prepared baking sheet, leaving a few inches between each one so that when they puff up in the oven they don't stick together.

Spoon 2 tablespoons of the cream into the saucepan of jam and stir until smooth. Then use the back of the spoon to spread the mixture evenly over each pastry, leaving a ½-inch margin all around the edges. Arrange the peach slices tightly over the jam so that they fit snugly and overlap. Take a sharp knife and cut a little slit (roughly ½ inch or 1cm) at each corner of the tarts, from the edge of the fruit to the very edge of the pastry. Then fold the corners in toward the center, pressing gently down where the pastry edges meet, so they stick together.

Crack the egg into a small cup, add the remaining 1 tablespoon cream, and whisk vigorously with a fork. Use a pastry brush to lightly glaze the edges of the pastry.

Set the baking sheet in the oven and bake for 25 to 30 minutes, until the pastries have puffed up and browned nicely, and the fruit looks tender to eat. The pastries are best eaten on the day of baking, while the fruit is still delicious and plump and before they become soggy.

APRICOT AND RAISIN STICKY PASTRIES

KRANZ

MAKES 8 PASTRIES

¾ cup / 100g raisins

¾ cup / 100g candied peel of choice

Juice of 1 orange

1 tablespoon brandy of choice

1 (17-ounce) package / 2 (320g) packages prepared puff pastry, thawed if frozen

⅔ cup / 200g apricot jam

1 large egg

⅓ cup / 60g granulated sugar

JUST LIKE THE KIEFER on page 33, kranz came to be a part of the Venetian way of eating when the Austrians occupied the city in the nineteenth century. These sticky pastries, laced with apricot jam and raisins, are now a beloved staple in bakeries, cafés, and pasticcerie across town.

Strictly speaking, kranz should be made by layering sheets of puff pastry with sheets of brioche dough, then twisting the two together. For sheer ease, I just use puff pastry—and the prepared variety at that. I do so with impunity, and find the result to be every bit as delightful as the finer pasticcerie counterpart.

Toss the raisins and the candied peel in a small bowl, pour in the orange juice and brandy, and let sit for 20 to 30 minutes.

Preheat the oven to 350°F. Line a baking sheet with parchment paper.

On a clean, cool surface, unfold the first sheet of pastry. Spread two-thirds of the jam on the pastry, going right up to the edges. Drain the raisins and candied peel, and sprinkle two-thirds over the jam.

Unfold the second sheet of pastry, gently lift it up, and drape it over the jam layer. Use a sharp knife to cut down the middle of the pastry, from top to bottom, dividing the sheet into 2 equal pieces. Spread the remaining jam over the top of one of the halves, top with the remaining raisins and candied peel, then top with the second filled pastry half. Cut the layered rectangle into strips roughly two fingers wide, and twist each strip on itself two to three times. The filling will ooze out slightly as you twist the pastry, but don't worry if it gets a little messy: the pastries are meant to look like they are bursting at the seams. Place the twists on the prepared baking sheet.

Crack the egg into a small bowl, lightly beat it, and use a pastry brush to glaze the pastries.

Bake for 20 to 25 minutes, until beautifully golden brown. Remove the sheet from the oven and let the pastries cool for 5 to 10 minutes.

Meanwhile, make a sugar syrup. Pour ¼ cup of water into a medium saucepan and add the sugar. Set over medium heat, bring to a simmer, and cook until the sugar has dissolved, 2 to 3 minutes. Use a pastry brush to brush the syrup on the cooling pastries. Eat while still sticky and warm, or leave to cool. (The kranz will keep in an airtight container for 2 to 3 days.)

CHOCOLATE AND ORANGE RICOTTA BREAKFAST CAKE

TORTA DI RICOTTA AL FIOR D'ARANCIO E CIOCCOLATO

SERVES 8 TO 10

FOR THE PASTRY

2⅓ cups / 300g all-purpose flour, plus more for dusting

A pinch of salt

⅔ cup / 150g cold salted butter, cut into cubes

FOR THE FILLING

2¾ cups / 650g whole-milk ricotta

⅔ cup / 80g confectioners' sugar

3 large eggs

Grated zest of 1 orange

6 ounces / 170g dark chocolate, roughly chopped

FOR THE GLAZE

1 large egg

WE CALL THIS *TORTA DI RICOTTA,* or ricotta cake, though for all intents and purposes it most closely resembles a cross between a cheesecake and a pie, with a lattice crust top. And while for those who don't have a sweet tooth it might seem like a step too far to begin the day with something so creamy, I can promise you that this cake is the exception. As a very distant cousin of the richer New York–style cheesecake, its light flavor and texture make it ideal for breakfast or any other time. Certainly there is nothing to stop you enjoying it for afternoon tea or after dinner for dessert as well—I often do. There is no need to make it first thing in the morning. It keeps very nicely for a few days in the fridge, and I find its flavors almost improve with a little time.

Begin by making the pastry. Sift the flour and salt into a large bowl. Use your fingers to rub the butter into the flour until the mixture has the consistency of coarse sand. Add 1 to 2 tablespoons of cold water to bring the dough together. (Even easier is to make the dough in a food processor. Pulse the flour and salt for a few seconds, then add the cold butter and process again until you have the consistency of sand. Remove the blade, add 1 to 2 tablespoons of cold water, and bring the dough together with your hands.) You want the dough to feel smooth and elastic, rather than sticky. If it feels too sticky, add a little more flour.

Roll the dough into a ball, wrap it in plastic wrap, and set it in the fridge to rest for 30 minutes, or overnight if you like.

Preheat the oven to 350°F.

Divide the pastry dough into 2 pieces, roughly two-thirds and one-third. On a lightly floured surface, roll out the larger piece into a disk to fit a 10-inch (28cm) tart pan. Gently lift the dough into the pan, press it into the bottom and edges, trim off the excess pastry, leaving a generous margin around the rim, and pierce the base a few times with a fork. Line the pastry with parchment paper and fill with baking beans or weights.

Bake the crust for 15 minutes, until the pastry feels dry to the touch, then remove the paper and baking beans, and bake for a further 5 minutes until very lightly colored. Remove from the oven and let cool slightly.

Meanwhile, make the filling. Spoon the ricotta through a sieve to drain away excess water. In a medium bowl, sift the confectioners' sugar into the ricotta and stir with a wooden spoon until smooth. Crack the 3 eggs into a small bowl, lightly beat with a fork, then stir them into the ricotta mixture. Fold in the orange zest and chocolate pieces.

Spoon the ricotta filling into the warm pastry shell. Use the back of your spoon to smooth the top. Roll out the remaining dough ball and cut it into strips that are about two fingers wide. Arrange the strips in a crisscross pattern over the top of the tart, seal the edges with moistened fingers, and trim away any excess pastry. Lightly beat the egg for the glaze in a small bowl with a fork, and use a pastry brush to lightly glaze the top of the tart.

Bake for 30 to 35 minutes, until the pastry is golden and the ricotta filling feels firm to the touch. Remove the tart from the oven and let cool for 10 to 15 minutes in its pan before taking it out, as the pastry can be a little crumbly when still hot. Serve warm or at room temperature. (The tart will keep in the refrigerator for up to 2 days.)

APPLE, HONEY, AND WALNUT CAKE

TORTA DI MELE, MIELE
E NOCI

SERVES 8 TO 10

4 to 5 medium dessert apples
(roughly 1¼ pounds / 600g)

3 large eggs

⅓ cup / 120g honey

½ cup / 125g plain whole-milk yogurt

3 tablespoons plus 1 teaspoon /
55ml olive oil

1¾ cups / 210g self-rising flour

Scant ½ cup / 50g walnut pieces

2 tablespoons / 30g salted butter

3 tablespoons / 35g light
brown sugar

EVERY ITALIAN MOTHER WORTH HER SALT has a recipe for apple cake, which she serves for breakfast and teatime alike. Venetian *mamme* are no exception. I am particularly fond of this version, made with a yogurt base and sweetened only with fresh fruit, a little honey, and a sprinkling of sugar to caramelize the top. It strikes that elusive balance between sweet treat and nourishing. As far as cakes go, it is also about as quick and simple to make as it gets: really just a matter of tossing ingredients into a bowl (I don't even bother peeling the apples) and mixing, which I find makes it wonderfully do-able, even first thing in the morning.

Preheat the oven to 350°F. Line a 9-inch (23cm) cake pan, preferably springform, with parchment paper.

Core the apples and roughly slice them lengthwise into half-moons. Roughly chop half the apple slices, and save the rest for decoration.

In a medium bowl, using a handheld mixer, whisk the eggs and honey vigorously for 2 to 3 minutes, until pale and fluffy. Add the yogurt and stir with a wooden spoon until well combined. Drizzle in the olive oil and stir until well combined. Sift the flour into the bowl and mix until there are no lumps. Toss in the chopped apple and walnuts, and give everything a good stir. Spoon the batter into the prepared cake pan, and use the back of the spoon to smooth the batter out evenly before arranging the remaining apple slices on the top of the cake. (I like to do this in a circle around the edge of the cake, but there's no rule.) Dab a few pieces of butter over the top of the cake, then sprinkle with the brown sugar.

Bake for 45 minutes, until golden brown on top. The cake should bounce back when you press down gently on the top center, and a knife or skewer inserted into the middle should come out clean. Eat warm or at room temperature. (It will keep in an airtight container for a few days.)

APPLE, RAISIN, PINE NUT, AND CINNAMON BREAD PUDDING

PINZA

MAKES 15 TO 20 SERVINGS

½ cup / 80g dried figs

¾ cup / 100g raisins

⅓ cup /50g candied peel of choice

3 tablespoons / 40ml brandy of choice

1 hefty loaf (1 pound / 500g) stale bread, tough crusts removed

4½ cups / 1L whole milk

½ cup / 90g granulated sugar

1 large egg

1 cup plus 3 tablespoons / 150g self-rising flour

1 teaspoon ground cinnamon

3 apples, cored

1 pear, cored

½ cup / 60g pine nuts

2 tablespoons / 30g salted butter

2 tablespoons light brown sugar

WHEN YOU COME FROM ONE PLACE and grow up in another, you tend to acquire traditions from both. One holiday tradition I've been happy to adopt is that of La Befana, which in Italy we celebrate on January 6, the day of Epiphany. La Befana is a witch; she flies on an old, bushy broomstick and leaves behind stockings filled with sweets—black-sugar coal if you've been naughty, and a hunk of white-sugar polenta if you've been nice. If you find yourself in Venice at that time of the year, you might be forgiven for confusing it with Halloween—there are witch decorations everywhere.

To celebrate La Befana, you traditionally make pinza: a bread pudding of sorts laced with fruit, raisins, candied peel, pine nuts, and in some cases either fennel seeds or almonds, or even a dash of chocolate. But pinza has come to be a dish that is enjoyed year-round: you will see it in bakeries for sale in large slabs, where you buy it by weight. It's rich and filling, and a small slice goes a long way. It's one of those recipes designed to use up leftovers, and while you can make it with yellow polenta, I prefer to use a mix of whole wheat and soft white bread. Use a good crusty bread that you might buy from the baker rather than a ready-sliced loaf, since it not only tastes better but also gives a more pleasing texture to the pudding.

Roughly chop the figs and toss them in a bowl along with the raisins and the candied peel. Pour in the brandy, cover the bowl with a clean tea towel, and let steep for 20 to 30 minutes.

Roughly tear the bread into pieces and place in a large bowl.

In a heavy-bottomed saucepan, warm the milk and sugar together over low heat for 2 to 3 minutes, until the sugar is completely dissolved. Pour the sweetened milk over the bread. Let steep for about 30 minutes, until most of the milk has been soaked up.

Preheat the oven to 350°F. Line a 10 by 8-inch (30 by 20cm) deep baking pan with parchment paper.

Add the egg, flour, and cinnamon to the milk-soaked bread and stir with a wooden spoon until well combined. Grate one of the apples, and roughly chop the pear, then add both to the bowl, along with the brandy-soaked fruits with their juices and the pine nuts. Stir well.

recipe continues

Spoon the pudding into the prepared baking dish, and level the top with the back of your spoon. Core and quarter the last 2 apples, then slice them into thin half-moons. Arrange the pieces of apple over the top of the pudding in any pattern you like. Chop the butter into small pieces and dab them here and there over the apple slices, then sprinkle with the brown sugar.

Bake for 1 hour, until firm to the touch and lightly golden on top. Serve warm or at room temperature. (The pudding will keep in an airtight container for 5 days.)

CHOCOLATE, ORANGE, AND HAZELNUT BREAKFAST BREAD

PUTIZZA

SERVES 8

FOR THE DOUGH

3¾ cups / 470g bread flour

⅓ cup / 70g granulated sugar

1 teaspoon salt

2 teaspoons instant yeast

Scant ⅓ cup / 70g salted butter, at room temperature

Scant 1 cup / 240ml whole milk

1 large egg

FOR THE FILLING

½ cup / 50g raisins

3 tablespoons / 40ml brandy of choice

Scant ⅓ cup / 70g salted butter, at room temperature

¼ cup / 50g light brown sugar

1¼ cups / 50g dry bread crumbs

2 tablespoons whole milk

2½ ounces / 75g dark chocolate, roughly chopped

½ cup / 75g roughly chopped blanched hazelnuts

Grated zest of 1 orange

FOR THE GLAZE

1 large egg

PUTIZZA, OR POTICA, IS A SLOVENIAN bread, which has over time made its way into the cannon of Venetian cooking. It is a deliciously soft, buttery bread (not unlike French brioche) that is filled with a thick paste of crushed nuts, chocolate, bread crumbs, and milk. I've use hazelnuts here and a touch of orange zest, but you could also use walnuts or almonds.

This recipe requires some time (for the dough to rest and rise) and a little patience (for kneading), but trust me: the joy that comes with a freshly baked loaf of sweet bread far and beyond exceeds the labor involved in the making of it. If you would like to eat it fresh from the oven in the morning, then make the dough the day before, fill and shape the loaf, cover the pan loosely with plastic wrap, and set the loaf to rise in the fridge overnight. The next day, take the loaf out of the fridge, bring it to room temperature, then glaze and bake.

First, get a head start on the filling. Combine the raisins and brandy in a small bowl, cover with a tea towel, and set to one side to allow the fruit to steep. The longer they soak, the plumper and more flavorsome the raisins will become.

To make the dough, sift the flour, sugar, and salt into a large bowl. Stir in the yeast. Use your fingers to rub the butter into the dry ingredients until there are no large lumps and the mixture has the texture of coarse sand. You can do this by pulsing the ingredients together in a food processor, if you prefer.

Gently warm the milk in a small saucepan for 1 to 2 minutes, until just above room temperature. Test the temperature by dripping a little milk on the underside of your wrist; it should feel warm, not uncomfortably hot. If the milk is too hot, it will kill the yeast and stop the bread from rising properly.

Make a well in the flour mixture, pour in the warm milk, and add the egg. Stir the dough, bringing the flour into the well, until incorporated. Knead the dough vigorously for 10 minutes or so, until it feels smooth and elastic. You can test to see if the dough is ready by tearing off a small piece and stretching it as thin as you can. If you can see light shining through the thinnest part of the dough, it is ready. Lightly oil a large bowl, shape the dough into a ball, roll it around to coat it with oil, and set it in the bowl. Cover with a damp tea towel, and place it somewhere warm to rise until doubled in size, about 1½ hours.

recipe continues

While the dough is rising, make the filling. In a medium bowl, beat the butter, sugar, and bread crumbs together with an electric mixer to form a thick paste. Pour in the milk and beat again until creamy and smooth. Stir in the chocolate and hazelnuts, then cover and set to one side.

Grease a 9-inch (23cm) cake pan, preferably springform, with butter. When the dough has doubled in size, tip it out of the bowl onto a work surface, and knock the air out of it. Take one-third of the dough and roll it out or stretch it to fit the bottom of your pan; this will form the bottom of the loaf.

On a lightly floured surface, roll out the rest of the dough into a large rectangle, roughly 12 by 9 inches (35 by 25cm). Stir the raisins and orange zest into the chocolate and hazelnut filling, and then spread the filling over the dough as evenly as you can right up to the edges. Roll it up from a long side until you have a giant sausage, then use a sharp knife to cut it into 8 to 10 slices, each roughly two to three fingers wide. Arrange the rounds snugly on top of the dough in the cake pan, swirly side up. Cover with a damp tea towel and set somewhere warm to rise a second time until nearly doubled in size again, this time about 45 minutes.

Preheat the oven to 350°F.

Just before putting the bread in the oven, in a small bowl, whisk the egg for the glaze with a fork and use a pastry brush to lightly glaze the top of the dough.

Bake for 40 to 45 minutes, until golden on top. If you insert a knife into the bread, it should come out clean and easily. This bread is particularly delightful to eat when still warm from the oven, but can also be enjoyed at room temperature. It is best when eaten on the day of baking.

FENNEL SEED AND CANDIED-PEEL YOGURT CAKE

CIAMBELLA ALLO YOGURT CON SEMI DI FINOCCHIO E CANDITI

SERVES 8

FOR THE CAKE

Unsalted butter, for greasing

3 large eggs

½ cup / 100g granulated sugar

½ cup / 135g plain whole-milk yogurt

3 tablespoons / 50ml olive oil

A pinch of salt

2¼ cups / 280g self-rising flour

1 teaspoon baking powder

½ cup / 60g candied peel of choice, chopped

1 tablespoon fennel seeds

FOR THE ICING

1⅔ cups / 200g confectioners' sugar

1 tablespoon orange blossom water

THIS IS THE SORT OF CAKE that even those who claim not to have a sweet tooth will enjoy eating for breakfast. It is sweet, but not too sweet, and lighter, both in taste and in texture, than most sponges—probably because it is made with yogurt and olive oil instead of butter. This is a staple that you will find at most Italian breakfast tables, usually baked as a *ciambella*—a ring shape, or what we might call a Bundt cake. Though I use a Bundt pan here, there's no need to buy one just to make this cake, as I have baked it just as often in a round 8-inch cake pan,

Feel free to play around with the flavors; make the cake plain, or throw in a half pint of raspberries, perhaps a handful of chocolate chunks, or raisins soaked in brandy. If you are planning on making it for breakfast, you might want to make the cake plain and just dust it with a little confectioners' sugar. But for afternoon tea, which is when I just as often end up eating this, I think there is something wonderfully decadent about a drizzle of white icing.

My only caveat: be patient when beating the eggs; take the time for them to froth up nicely, and your patience will be rewarded with a crumb that is deliciously light.

Preheat the oven to 350°F. Grease a 10-inch (1L) Bundt pan with butter.

To make the cake, in a large bowl, beat the eggs and sugar vigorously until they become light, fluffy, and pale in color, 3 to 5 minutes. Add the yogurt, olive oil, and salt; stir with a wooden spoon until well combined. Sift in the flour and the baking powder, then stir until smooth. Gently fold in the candied peel and two-thirds of the fennel seeds, then pour the batter into the prepared pan. If the batter doesn't seem enough at this point, don't worry; it should only fill about two-thirds of the pan.

Set the pan on the middle rack and bake for 20 to 25 minutes, until lightly golden on top and a knife or skewer inserted into the middle of the cake comes out clean. If you press down gently on the top of the cake with your finger, it should spring back. Turn the cake out onto a cooling rack.

If you're planning to ice the cake, allow it to cool completely. Sift the confectioners' sugar into a small bowl. Slowly add the orange blossom water (and a little cold water, if needed), stirring vigorously all the while with a spoon to stop lumps from forming. You want the icing to be runny, but not so thin that it won't set; when you hold up the spoon, the icing should trickle off slowly like runny honey. If the icing is too thick, add a little more water, and if it becomes too runny, sift in a touch more sugar. Use a teaspoon to drizzle the icing over the cake, and sprinkle with the rest of the fennel seeds for decoration.

FIG AND MASCARPONE CAKE

TORTA DI MASCARPONE
E FICHI

SERVES 8 TO 10

1 cup plus 1 tablespoon /
250g mascarpone

⅞ cup / 180g granulated sugar

3 large eggs

2 cups / 250g self-rising flour

1 teaspoon baking powder

A pinch of salt

8 fresh figs, stemmed and quartered

1 tablespoon confectioners' sugar

THE BOUNTY OF FIGS IS POSSIBLY one of the things I love most about late summer in Venice. We have a fig tree in our garden, and it bears more fruit than we can possibly eat—or so you'd think. We always seem to find a way of finishing them off.

Nothing quite compares to this cake in the heat of summer. While you can make it out of season with dried figs, it doesn't quite hold the same magic as when laced with luscious fresh fruit; nevertheless, the dried variety produces a pretty fine substitute on a cold winter's day. Use 12 to 14 dried figs, cut away the tough stems, toss them in a small saucepan, and cover with a little over ½ cup (130ml) milk. Simmer gently on medium to low heat for 5 to 10 minutes, until the figs have softened, then let steep in the milk for a further 15 to 20 minutes. Drain the milk and quarter the figs before adding to the batter as you would the fresh fruit.

Preheat the oven to 350°F. Line a 9-inch (23cm) cake pan, preferably springform, with parchment paper.

In a large bowl, beat the mascarpone, granulated sugar, and eggs until you have a smooth, thick cream. Sift in the flour, baking powder, and salt, and stir with a wooden spoon until well combined. Gently stir in the quartered figs. Spoon the batter into the prepared pan.

Bake for 40 to 45 minutes, until lightly golden on top and a knife or skewer inserted into the middle of the cake comes out clean. When you press down on the top of the cake, it should spring back nicely. Let cool for 10 to 15 minutes in the pan before taking it out to cool. Dust lightly with confectioners' sugar and cut into slices to serve.

SUGAR BUNS

FOCACCINE VENEZIANE

MAKES 8 SMALL BUNS

¼ cup / 50ml whole milk

1 cup (2 sticks) / 250g salted butter, chopped

1 tablespoon wildflower honey

6 large eggs

4 cups / 500g bread flour

½ cup / 100g granulated sugar

A generous pinch of salt

2 teaspoons / 7g instant yeast

WHEN YOU HEAR FOCACCIA, you most likely think of the savory variety (see page 73), which is eaten across Italy but originally comes from the town of Genova in Liguria, on the northeastern coast of Italy. These soft, sweet buns, made with milk and honey and topped with a glistening crust of sugar, are what we call Venetian focaccia. The dough is very rich, richer than most brioche bread—made with a lot of eggs that give it the most deliciously delicate yellow color. You will find these for sale in bakeries across town, but they are very hard to source outside of Venice—unless, of course, you bake your own.

In a small saucepan, warm the milk, butter, and honey over a gentle heat until the butter is just melted. The liquid should be lukewarm but not scalding—you should be able to comfortably hold your finger in it.

In a small bowl, lightly beat five of the eggs with a fork. Set aside.

Sift the flour, ⅓ cup (65g) of the sugar, and the salt into a large bowl, and then stir in the yeast. Pour the warm milk mixture and the beaten eggs into the flour mixture, and combine to form a dough. Turn the dough out onto a clean, lightly floured surface and knead until smooth and elastic, 8 to 10 minutes. If you tear a small piece of dough off, stretch it out and hold it up to the light; you should be able to see the shadow of something on the other side.

Wash out and lightly grease the bowl with oil. Roll the dough into a ball, roll it around the bowl to lightly coat it, and cover with plastic wrap or a damp tea towel and set somewhere warm to rise until doubled in size, 1 to 1½ hours.

Line a baking sheet with parchment paper. When the dough has risen, knock it back with your knuckles, and shape it into 8 small, smooth balls roughly the size of a large apricot. Arrange them on the prepared sheet, allowing a little space between each ball of dough, as they will puff up as they rise and bake. Cover with plastic wrap and set somewhere warm to rise until nearly doubled in size, 45 minutes to 1 hour.

Preheat the oven to 350°F.

In a small bowl, lightly beat the remaining egg and use a pastry brush to glaze the top of each bun. Sprinkle the tops of the buns generously with the remaining sugar.

Bake for 20 to 25 minutes, until the buns are lightly golden on top and sound hollow if you tap them on the bottom. The buns are best eaten on the day you bake them.

JAM DAISY COOKIES

MARGHERITE ALLA
MARMELLATA

MAKES 30 COOKIES

2⅓ cups / 300g all-purpose flour,
plus more for dusting

1 cup / 120g confectioners' sugar

A pinch of salt

1 teaspoon baking powder

½ cup (1 stick) / 125g chilled
salted butter

1 large egg

6 tablespoons / 120g smooth
apricot jam

THESE REMIND ME OF WHAT IN ENGLAND you might call "Jammy Dodgers," only the cookies are sweeter, more buttery, and closer to short-bread. Sandwiched between them is apricot jam, though some *pasticcerie* replace the jam with a thin layer of melted dark chocolate. In Italy we call these *margherite*, which you might loosely translate as "daisy cookies" because of their shape, I think, which has something of an unassuming cheerful flower about it. Either way, they make a very nice start to the day, not least when dipped into hot chocolate or a cup of warm milk. My son, Aeneas, has a couple of these for breakfast every morning.

Sift the flour, sugar, salt, and baking powder together into a large bowl. Use your fingers to rub the butter into the dry ingredients until the mixture has the consistency of coarse sand. (Alternatively, use a food processor: pour in the dry ingredients [no need to sift], pulse for 30 seconds or so, then add the butter and process until you have the consistency of coarse sand.)

Crack the egg in a small bowl, lightly beat with a fork, and add it to your flour mixture. Use your hands to bring everything together into a smooth dough. If the dough feels too crumbly, you can add a tablespoon of cold water. It should feel smooth in your hands. Roll the dough into a ball, wrap it in plastic wrap, and set it in the fridge to chill for 30 minutes, or overnight.

When you are ready to bake, preheat the oven to 400°F. Line a baking sheet with parchment paper.

On a lightly floured surface, roll out your dough to roughly ¼ inch in thickness. Use a 1½–inch (38mm) round cookie cutter (ideally with a frilly edge) to cut out the shapes and arrange them a little apart on the baking sheet. Take a smaller round (ideally also frilly edged) cookie cutter to cut a small hole in the center of half the circles, so that each whole circle can be paired with one with a hole. (If you can't find a cutter small enough to make the hole, use a sharp knife to trace a little hole freehand.) Reroll the scraps to get as many cookies as you can out of the dough; you should have about 30 of each shape.

Bake for 8 to 10 minutes, until lightly golden. Transfer the cookies to a cooling rack and let cool for 15 to 20 minutes. Spoon a little apricot jam (half a teaspoon is probably enough; a little goes a long way) on top of each whole cookie and top with a cookie with a small hole, making a sandwich. (The cookies will keep in an airtight container for 3 to 5 days.)

POLENTA AND RAISIN COOKIES

ZALETTI

MAKES 40 COOKIES

¾ cup / 100g raisins

1 tablespoon / 20ml grappa or other eau-de-vie

Scant 2 cups / 300g fine polenta

1⅔ cups / 200g all-purpose flour

1 teaspoon baking powder

A pinch of salt

¾ cup / 150g granulated sugar

1 tablespoon / 15ml whole milk

½ cup (1 stick) / 100g salted butter

1 large egg

YOU COULD JUST AS WELL have these after dinner with coffee, a glass of sweet wine, or a sharp grappa—and, in fact, that is what we often do. But growing up, I would eat these dipped in milk for breakfast. They are made with polenta flour, which gives them both the deep yellow color and their name *zaletti*, which in Venetian dialect translates loosely to "little yellow ones."

Preheat the oven to 350°F. Line a baking sheet with parchment paper.

In a small bowl, combine the raisins and grappa, give it a stir, then cover with a clean tea towel. Let steep while you make the cookie dough.

Pour the polenta, flour, baking powder, and salt into a large bowl. Stir in the sugar.

In a small saucepan set over low heat, heat the milk and butter until the butter is melted, 1 to 2 minutes. Pour the warm milk into the dry ingredients and give everything a good stir with a wooden spoon. Crack the egg into a small bowl and beat lightly with a fork, then pour into the mixture. Use your hands to bring the dough together. Drain the raisins and mix them into the dough.

Take a heaping teaspoonful of dough and shape it into a small round, like a walnut, then set it on the prepared baking sheet; repeat with the remaining dough, allowing a little space between the balls on the sheet.

Bake for 10 to 12 minutes, until lightly golden. Transfer to a rack and allow to cool completely. (These will keep in an airtight container for up to 1 week.)

THICK HOT CHOCOLATE WITH ZABAIONE

CIOCCOLATA CALDA CON ZABAIONE

SERVES 4

FOR THE ZABAIONE
(OPTIONAL)

2 large egg yolks

2½ tablespoons /
30g granulated sugar

2 tablespoons / 25ml Marsala wine

FOR THE HOT CHOCOLATE

¼ cup / 20g unsweetened
cocoa powder

3 tablespoons /
35g granulated sugar

3 teaspoons cornstarch

2 cups / 450ml whole milk

A DOLLOP OF ZABAIONE in this thick, dark hot chocolate is sheer indulgence, and while perhaps it is borderline a-little-too-much for breakfast on a weekday, it is sheer bliss when you need an afternoon pick-me-up in the depths of cold winter. That said, the hot chocolate, which is somewhere between a rich drinking chocolate and a custard, stands beautifully on its own, too.

If you're making the zabaione, fill a saucepan one-third full with cold water and bring to a boil, then reduce the heat. Choose a heatproof bowl that fits snugly over the saucepan without the bottom touching the water, or the eggs will cook. Put the egg yolks and sugar into the bowl. Using a handheld mixer, whisk until deliciously light and fluffy, 2 to 3 minutes (a little longer if you are beating it by hand). Set the bowl over the simmering water, and gently heat while whisking constantly. Slowly pour the Marsala into the frothy egg cream, little by little, whisking all the while. This should take 5 to 7 minutes, and as you add the liquid, the zabaione will double in size and thicken. Set it to one side or chill in the fridge.

To make the hot chocolate, in a medium saucepan, combine the cocoa powder, sugar, cornstarch, and milk and give everything a good stir. Set the saucepan over low heat and cook, stirring constantly with a wooden spoon, for 1 to 2 minutes, until you have a smooth chocolatey milk. Now turn up the heat to medium, and keep stirring for 4 to 5 minutes, until the chocolate becomes thick and custardy. Remove the pan from the heat and pour into 4 small cups. Top with a dollop of zabaione, if you like.

PEACH
ICED TEA

THÉ FREDDO ALLA PESCA

MAKES A LARGE JUG OF ICED TEA

English Breakfast tea

1 to 2 tablespoons sugar

1 ripe peach

ICED TEA IS MADE NO DIFFERENTLY from regular tea: boiling water is poured over a teabag and left to steep, then sweetened with a spoonful of sugar. But just as hot tea has an almost uncanny knack for making you feel better on a cold winter's day, a tall glass of iced tea is a wonderfully refreshing way to start the day in the sweltering heat of summer. You can infuse iced tea with pretty much whatever strikes your fancy: wedges of lemon, fresh garden mint, or even lemon verbena—all are favorites of mine. But peach has a delicate sweetness to it that I find irresistible.

Make a pot of very weak tea. Add sugar, and stir until dissolved. Halve the peach, discard the stone, and cut the peach into half-moon slices. Throw the peach slices into the tea, and leave to cool to room temperature. Then refrigerate until cold. Serve over ice.

IL MERCATO

VEGETABLE RECIPES
FROM THE RIALTO MARKET

AT THE HEART OF LIFE IN VENICE is *il mercato*, the Rialto Market. This cluster of stalls nestles at the foot of the Rialto Bridge, under the archway and looking out over the Grand Canal–the same place the market has stood for hundreds of years. Here you'll find fruit, vegetables, cheeses, fish, meat, breads, and spices. *Il mercato* is bustling and loud, and as much a social as a culinary center. For the person who loves to eat, it is a scene of irresistible plenty.

Like most Venetians, I shop there daily, as supermarkets are few and far between in the city. I go early, because by noon everything has wound down, the traders having packed up and headed home to enjoy lunch with their families. I buy only what I need to cook for that day because, with no car to load my shopping into, that is about as much as I can carry in my basket over the bridges back to our house in sleepy Castello. And I buy seasonal and local produce, not so much out of any great desire to adhere to current trends but because that is what there is to buy. You won't find kiwis or mangos at the Rialto Market, though in winter, there are piles upon piles of wine-colored radicchio and come spring, baby artichokes–the ones so tender you can eat their petals raw–are heaped high on the stands.

Swooping seagulls, raspy voices haggling in dialect, beautiful fruit and vegetables like something out of a Caravaggio painting–there's little about shopping at the Rialto that is modern, yet I wouldn't trade the romance of the market, with its many quirks, for any store, however convenient. I paint this picture for you because *il mercato* shapes the way I cook.

What makes the Italian diet a largely healthy one is the sheer preponderance of vegetables, cooked and served every which way, both at lunch and at dinner. But what makes it such a nourishing, gratifying diet is the way vegetables are celebrated and imbue the dining table with vibrant, irresistible, plentiful color. It is vegetables, the fruits of *il mercato*, in all their glorious simplicity, that are the theme of this chapter.

While by convention we might be tempted to label these dishes "sides," I urge you not to confine them to a secondary role: they are stars in their own right. This is the kind of food that you can eat as you please–mix and match; pair with fish or meat, pasta, or risotto; serve as starters; or combine to build a delightful meal. In some ways this chapter is an anomaly: it doesn't conform to a single meal; it is for all meals.

A large part of the charm of shopping at *il mercato*, of course, is the vendors who sell the goods. The stalls are all small, family-run businesses. Italians do vegetables well, and naturally, this starts with the source. Many grow their own produce in gardens on the nearby island of Sant'Erasmo—like Neni, who, year after year, has the most vibrantly hued zucchini flowers, or Giovanna, who somehow always manages to be the first to stock bruscandoli (a kind of wild hops foraged in the lagoon that you cook and use as you might asparagus) each spring. Shopping there over the years, a cook gets to know each seller well, just as they get to know you. Some are grumpy, most are brusque, but they are universally passionate about the food they sell.

No vendor at the market will let you take a bag of artichoke hearts home without pressing into your hands a bunch of fresh parsley to fry in the pan with them. They won't give you a pumpkin without first inquiring how you intend to eat it; then they will, with care, choose the right kind for you, according to whether you're making soup, ravioli, or cooking it *in saor*, say. A heated conversation about whether to pair the pumpkin with rosemary or sage might ensue; and you will leave the stall not just with your squash but also with the herbs and the garlic and whatever else you might need to go with it, along with strict instructions on how much salt or butter to use, thoughts on how the vendor prefers to eat it, and notes on how his mother cooks it.

When you go back for your shopping the next day, he will ask how it was, taking little mind of the bustling line of customers waiting behind you. This can be at once invigorating and frustrating, largely depending on where you are in that line. It certainly means that there is little that is fast about shopping or food—but then come to think of it, that's true of life, too—in Venice.

OLIVE FOCACCIA BREAD

**MAKES 2 MEDIUM LOAVES
(EACH LOAF SERVES 6 TO 8 PEOPLE)**

4 cups / 500g bread flour,
plus more for dusting

———

2 teaspoons fine salt, plus
more for sprinkling

———

1 tablespoon / 10g instant yeast

———

2 tablespoons olive oil, plus
more for drizzling

———

1⅔ cups / 400ml cold water

———

16 to 20 green olives, pitted

I COULDN'T START THIS CHAPTER without including a recipe for a good loaf of bread: it is what brings a meal together. Many of the very best bread bakeries in Venice are clustered around the Rialto Market, which means I can easily pick up bread when I buy my fruit, vegetables, spices, and fish. That said, nothing compares with a homemade loaf.

Focaccia is an excellent bread to make at home, as it's hard to go wrong with it and it's delectable to eat. I have topped this one with briny olives, which are a lovely, salty complement to the soft, doughy bread. However, you could try replacing the olives with baby tomatoes, or just drizzle it copiously with oil, then sprinkle it with salt and chopped fresh rosemary or thyme.

———

In a large bowl, combine the flour, salt, yeast, 2 tablespoons olive oil, and the water, and stir with a wooden spoon until well combined. Transfer the dough to a floured surface and knead until it is smooth and elastic, about 10 minutes. If you give the dough a strong poke with your finger, it should bounce back quickly; if it doesn't, knead it a little while longer. If the dough feels too sticky as you are working it, then add a little more flour. Shape the dough into a large ball.

Wash the bowl, lightly grease it with a little olive oil, and put the ball of dough in it, turning it a bit to lightly coat with the oil. Cover the bowl with a clean, damp tea towel or plastic wrap and set it somewhere warm for the dough to rise for 1 hour, or until doubled in size.

When the dough has risen, transfer it to a floured surface, knock it down, and knead it for a couple of minutes. Divide the dough in half.

Lightly grease 2 small baking sheets with olive oil, and put one piece of dough on each sheet. Pull and stretch the dough into circles or ovals 1½ to 2 inches thick, then cover it with tea towels and set it somewhere warm for the bread to rise for 1 more hour, or until doubled in size.

Preheat the oven to 400°F.

When you are ready to bake the bread, use your fingers to press hollows into the top of the dough, drizzle it with a couple of tablespoons of olive oil, nestle the olives into the holes, and sprinkle generously with salt. Bake for 20 minutes, until each loaf is golden on top; reverse the sheets if they are browning unevenly. Test if the loaves are done by gently lifting one up and tapping on its underside with a knife or your knuckles; it should make a light hollow sound.

Focaccia is particularly delicious when warm from the oven, but in any event should really be eaten within 24 hours of baking.

PAN-FRIED ARTICHOKE HEARTS WITH PARSLEY

FONDI DI CARCIOFO CON PREZZEMOLO

SERVES 6, AS A STARTER

6 globe artichokes

1 lemon

1 tablespoon salted butter

2 tablespoons olive oil

1 garlic clove, peeled

Small bunch of fresh parsley, roughly chopped

Salt and freshly ground black pepper

½ cup / 150ml vegetable broth

IN VENICE, YOU WILL FIND ARTICHOKE HEARTS, already cleaned and ready to go, for sale at most markets. If you go to the market early enough, you will see the vendors cutting away the petals with a speed and fury that is hypnotic to watch, then tossing each heart into a bucket of cold water with lemon slices to stop them from browning. Perhaps because they are so readily available, I have come to think of artichoke hearts as a fast food—an easy dish, for which all I need to do is toss them in the pan with a little butter, oil, stock, and parsley, and I'm done. Prepping the artichokes yourself, of course, is a more laborious process, but by no means tricky or time-consuming once you've got the hang of it.

To prepare the artichokes, snap off the outer, tougher leaves. Work your way around the artichoke until the leaves begin to feel soft to the touch and become paler in color. Now, use a sharp paring knife to trim away the green skin around the base of the artichoke and the stem, then cut across the artichoke just below the point where the leaves meet the heart. Then cut across the bottom of the artichoke so you are left with a thick, flat disk. Discard all the leaves and scoop out the remaining choke. As you work, toss the cleaned hearts into a large bowl of water with a squeeze of lemon. (You can do this ahead of time, if you like, and leave them in the cold acidulated water for up to 1 day.)

Spoon the butter and olive oil into a large frying pan and add the garlic. Set over medium heat for a minute or so, until the butter has melted. Now add the artichoke hearts, face down, and gently cook for 3 to 5 minutes until browned, turning them so they color lightly on both sides. Add the parsley, and season with a little salt and pepper. Pour in the broth, cover the pan, and let cook for about 20 minutes, until the artichokes become tender; if you pierce them with a paring knife, you should feel very little resistance.

Lift the lid, turn the artichokes over, and pan-fry until all the stock has evaporated, about 10 minutes. Serve hot or at room temperature. (The cooked artichokes will keep in an airtight container in the fridge for 2 days.)

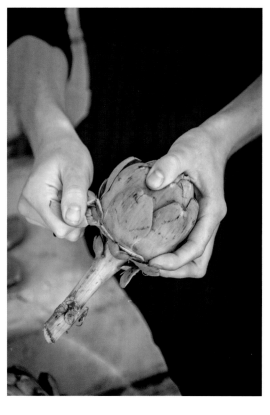

SPINACH WITH PINE NUTS AND RAISINS

SPINACI CON PINOLI
E UVETTA

SERVES 4 TO 6

2 tablespoons olive oil

2 garlic cloves, thinly sliced

1¾ pounds / 800g fresh spinach,
tough stems trimmed

¼ cup / 40g pine nuts

2 tablespoons / 30g salted butter

½ cup / 50g raisins

1 lemon

A generous pinch of Maldon
or kosher salt

Freshly ground black pepper

UNLIKE MY SPINACH, RICOTTA, AND MINT PIE (page 111), which is made with frozen spinach, this recipe calls for fresh spinach leaves. It relies on their strong flavor and their rich texture.

The Venetian touch is the addition of sweet raisins and lightly roasted pine nuts, a recurring theme in traditional Venetian cooking. Here they add a subtle sweetness that is entirely complementary to the slight bitterness of the green leaves. This is a dish you can serve with pretty much anything.

Set a large frying pan over medium heat until hot. Add the olive oil and garlic. Cook, shaking the pan around so the garlic cooks evenly, and taking care not to burn it, until the garlic turns golden, 1 to 2 minutes. Add the spinach in batches and move it around a little with a wooden spoon. Don't worry if it looks like too much spinach for the pan; it will wilt down quickly. Cook for a minute or so, until the spinach has cooked down, then remove the pan from the heat. Transfer the spinach to a colander to drain excess liquid.

Spread out the pine nuts in a single layer on the bottom of a large skillet. Set over medium-low heat and toast, stirring frequently, until golden, 2 to 3 minutes. Set aside.

Put the large saucepan that you cooked the spinach in back over medium heat. Add the butter and when the butter is melted, toss the spinach back in and add the raisins. Squeeze in the lemon juice, season with salt and pepper to taste, and give everything a good stir. Add the pine nuts, toss well, and eat immediately.

ROASTED CELERY WITH CHERRY TOMATOES AND PANCETTA

SEDANO AL FORNO

SERVES 4

Maldon or kosher salt

½ lemon

1 head of celery, with 8 to 10 stalks

3 tablespoons / 50ml olive oil

½ medium onion, chopped

⅔ cup / 100g cubed pancetta

1 pound / 450g cherry tomatoes, halved

Freshly ground black pepper

I WAS NEVER ABLE TO GET myself hugely excited about celery; it's a veg-etable I tend to think of as relegated to a supporting role in the kitchen—the basis of a good soffritto, perhaps, but not something I would cook or eat on its own. Then I tried eating it this way—poached in salted water until slightly tender, then roasted in the oven with cherry tomatoes and crisp salty pancetta. The result is almost ridiculously good. No less so because it is so simple to make. This dish is best served hot from the oven, though I have been known to greedily eat up leftovers straight from the fridge the next day.

Preheat the oven to 350°F.

Bring a large pot of water to a boil, then add 1 heaping teaspoon of salt and squeeze in the juice of half a lemon. Break the celery stalks free from the head and trim off the leaves. Add the whole celery stalks and simmer for 10 to 12 minutes, until they feel slightly tender when pierced with a fork. Drain and arrange in a medium roasting pan.

Set a medium frying pan over medium heat, and add 1 tablespoon of the olive oil. Then add the onion and pancetta. Cook, stirring, until the pancetta is crisp and the onion is translucent, 4 to 5 minutes. Spoon the pancetta and onion, along with the cooking juices, over the celery. Toss the tomatoes into the dish also, then drizzle with the remaining 2 tablespoons olive oil. Sprinkle generously with salt and pepper, and cover the tray with aluminum foil.

Roast for 1 hour. Remove the foil and continue roasting for another 10 to 15 minutes, until very lightly colored. Serve hot.

NONNA'S PEAS

I PISELLI DELLA NONNA

SERVES 4 TO 6

1 tablespoon olive oil

2 medium onions, finely chopped

3½ cups / 500g frozen peas

¾ cup / 180ml vegetable broth

A generous pinch of salt

Freshly ground black pepper

WITH THIS RECIPE, I HAVE STRAYED from the Rialto into the realm of the frozen goods aisle of the supermarket, but this way of cooking peas is so very dear to my heart that I couldn't not include the recipe for it. It is what I grew up eating, and it remains one of my favorite ways to eat peas. The recipe calls for frozen peas, to which you add a little onion and then drench in a good vegetable stock, so that you end up with a dish bursting with flavor. This is my go-to when I am craving something comforting and easy, and it goes just as beautifully with fish as with meat. If I have any leftovers, I toss them with pasta the next day, adding a little cream and pan-fried pancetta.

Set a medium saucepan over medium heat, add the oil and chopped onions, and cook for 5 to 10 minutes, until the onions begin to turn translucent.

Add the peas and cook until they begin to turn a more vibrant shade of green, 1 to 2 minutes. Then pour in the broth. Season with a little salt and pepper, reduce the heat, and simmer until all the liquid has been absorbed, about 10 minutes. Give everything a good stir before serving.

CREAM OF PUMPKIN SOUP

CREMA DI ZUCCA

SERVES 4 TO 6

4⅓ cups / 1L beef or chicken stock

3 tablespoons / 50ml olive oil

1 medium onion, chopped

Maldon or kosher salt

2½ pounds / 1.2kg pumpkin, peeled, seeded, and medium chopped

Freshly ground black pepper

¼ teaspoon ground nutmeg (optional)

¼ teaspoon ground cinnamon (optional)

I FIRST HAPPENED UPON THIS RECIPE in an old Venetian cookbook called *A Tòla co i Nostri Veci*, and it has fast become a favorite during the autumn and winter, when I crave food that feels indulgent and warming. The secret is to start with a good pumpkin, ideally a small one between 2 and 3 pounds (1 to 2kg), as they tend to have the most flavor. And if you can't find pumpkin, use butternut squash instead. I've used beef stock here because I find it deliciously flavorful, but you can substitute a good vegetable stock and just add a pinch more salt.

If you fancy a special treat, sprinkle a few crumbled amaretti over the soup just before serving. I learned this trick from my mother, who serves it this way for fancy dinner parties, though I'll do it when I'm by myself, enjoying a bowl of soup while relaxing on the sofa.

Pour the stock into a medium saucepan. Set the pan over medium heat and bring to a boil.

In a large pot heat the oil over medium heat, then add the onion, and a generous pinch of salt. Cook, stirring, until the onion becomes translucent, about 5 to 10 minutes. Add the pumpkin and stir well so that everything is nicely coated in olive oil. Pour in the boiling stock and bring back to a boil. Lower the heat to medium-low and simmer until the pumpkin has become soft and tender, 15 to 20 minutes. Test to see if it is done by piercing it with a fork.

Remove the pot from the heat and use a handheld blender to puree the mixture until it is silky and smooth, or puree in batches in a stand blender. Season with salt and pepper to taste, and add the nutmeg and cinnamon, if using.

Serve immediately while still hot, perhaps with a drizzle of olive oil and a few crumbled amaretti. (The soup will keep in an airtight container in the fridge for 3 days.)

RICOTTA AND MINT-STUFFED ZUCCHINI FLOWERS

FIORI DI ZUCCA RIPIENI
CON RICOTTA E MENTA

SERVES 4, AS A STARTER

⅓ cup / 70g ricotta

Small bunch of fresh mint,
finely chopped

Maldon or kosher salt

8 zucchini (squash) flowers

7 tablespoons / 100g Italian
"type 00" flour or all-purpose flour

⅔ cup / 150ml sparkling water

½ tablespoon olive oil

Peanut oil, for frying

ZUCCHINI FLOWERS COOKED THIS WAY are the biggest treat—partly because the blossoms are in season for such a short time, but mostly because they are just so blissfully indulgent to eat. In fact, this is one of very few dishes that I will, out of sheer greed, happily go to the effort of cooking only for myself. These must—categorically must—be eaten while still piping hot and deliciously light; they don't sit around well, which is why they are a dish that I like to cook for small numbers or in batches when I can easily cook and chat at the same time.

If you are unused to deep-frying, the process can seem a little daunting at first. If you don't have a deep-fat fryer, use a deep pot that will allow for a good few inches between the top of the pot and the top of the oil so as to avoid any splashing (the pot should be no more than a third or half full). Also choose a pot with a heavy bottom so that the oil heats up evenly. I have used what in Italy is called "tipo 00" flour, a refined flour that ensures the batter will be as light as can be. It is available online, but if you cannot find it, substitute all-purpose flour.

In a small bowl, combine the ricotta, mint, and a generous pinch of salt.

Gently pry open the petals of each squash blossom, tear out and discard the stamen, then spoon in a teaspoon of the ricotta mixture. Twist the petals to enclose the filling and set aside.

Sift the flour into a medium bowl. Whisk in the sparkling water, olive oil, and ½ teaspoon salt until you have a smooth, light batter.

Fill a deep-frying pot half full with peanut oil, and heat to 375°F. To test if the oil is ready, toss a small piece of bread into the pot; it should turn golden and crisp up within 30 seconds; if the bread browns much quicker than this, then the oil is too hot and you need to turn the heat down a little and test again.

One by one, drop each squash blossom by its stem into the batter, roll it around so it is evenly covered, lift it out, and let any excess batter drip off. Then drop the blossom into the hot oil. Fry until uniformly golden brown, about 2 minutes. Immediately use a slotted spoon to lift the flower out of the oil and set it on a sheet of paper towel to drain. Repeat with the remaining flowers. Sprinkle them with some salt and eat while still piping hot.

GRATIN OF FENNEL

FINOCCHIO AL LATTE

SERVES 4 TO 6

4 fennel bulbs, with some tops

3½ tablespoons / 50g salted butter

1¼ cups / 300ml whole milk

3 or 4 bay leaves

Salt and freshly ground black pepper

1 cup / 90g grated Parmesan cheese

½ cup / 30g coarse fresh
bread crumbs

THIS IS FOOD FOR COLD DAYS when you're craving comfort and warmth. The fennel is lightly poached in milk, smothered in melted cheese and butter, and topped with crisp bread crumbs that turn beautifully golden with baking. I think it's a lighter, though still indulgent, alternative to potatoes, and it pairs very well with anything from roasted meat to grilled fish.

A lighter version of this dish (and one which I am particularly partial to in the summer months) is to slice the fennel bulbs into rounds (roughly 1 inch thick) and arrange them on a baking sheet. Top each slice with a couple tablespoons of grated Parmesan and bake in a moderate oven for 30 minutes, until the cheese is golden and melted, and the fennel has tenderized nicely.

Preheat the oven to 425°F.

Trim and quarter the fennel bulbs, slicing them vertically, from top to bottom. Set the leafy fronds to one side to garnish the dish later. Slice the lengthwise chunks of fennel into thirds lengthwise again.

Melt half the butter in a medium ovenproof frying pan or casserole dish over medium heat. When the butter is melted, toss in the fennel and fry gently until it begins to color a little, 3 to 5 minutes. Pour in the milk, add the bay leaves, and let simmer over low heat for 10 minutes or so, giving it a good stir from time to time, until almost all the milk has evaporated and there's only a little bit left on the bottom of the pan. Remove the pan from the heat. Season with a little salt and pepper, then sprinkle the grated cheese and bread crumbs over. Cut the remaining butter into small pieces and dab them over the top of the dish.

Bake for 20 minutes, until golden brown. Roughly tear the fennel fronds and sprinkle liberally over the dish before serving.

BUTTER BEANS WITH SAGE

FAGIOLINI BIANCHI CON SALVIA

SERVES 6 AS A SIDE DISH, OR 4 AS A MAIN COURSE

2⅓ cups / 400g dried butter beans

A large bunch of fresh sage

1 heaping teaspoon salt, plus more for sprinkling

2 tablespoons olive oil

2 tablespoons / 25g salted butter

1 medium onion, finely chopped

Freshly ground black pepper

I FIND THE SIMPLE RITUAL of cooking these to be every bit as gratifying as that of eating them: there is something about the way the kitchen fills with the scent of sage as the beans bubble away that is deeply pleasing. This dish is very good to eat alongside fish or meat, or my particular favorite is to serve it on crusty bread, rather like a grown-up version of the British favorite, baked beans on toast.

The cooking begins the night before with soaking the beans in cold water; this requires almost no effort, but does call for some forethought. If you forget, you can boil the beans for two minutes in boiling water and then leave them to stand in their cooking water for one to two hours, before draining, rinsing, and cooking as usual. A couple of tips when cooking the beans: never let them boil except at the very beginning, but cook them on a gentle simmer so they stay whole and creamy; only add the salt halfway through cooking, when they are a little tenderized, so they better absorb the flavor.

Put the beans in a large pot, cover them with a few inches of water, and let them soak overnight. Drain and rinse. Return the beans to the pot and cover with a few inches of fresh water. Set the pot over medium heat, bring to a boil, and toss in half the sage. Reduce the heat and simmer until the beans begin to feel tender, about 45 minutes. Add the salt and simmer until the beans are soft, 30 more minutes. They should feel tender to press between your fingers; taste a few beans, too, as some might be more cooked through than others.

Meanwhile, heat the olive oil and butter in a medium skillet set over medium heat. Add the onion and a pinch of salt, and cook, stirring, until the onion begins to turn translucent, 5 to 10 minutes. Tear the leaves off the remaining sage sprigs and add them to the skillet. Cook, stirring, until the sage leaves begin to crisp, 3 to 5 minutes, then set aside.

Drain the beans, remove and discard the sage, and then toss the beans into a large bowl. Add the onion mixture and stir well. You can add a little extra oil if the beans seem dry, then season with salt and pepper to taste. Serve warm or at room temperature.

GARDEN PEA AND ALMOND SALAD

INSALATA DI PISELLI E MANDORLE

SERVES 6

Salt

6 cups / 600g shelled peas

6 tablespoons / 80ml olive oil

A handful of blanched almonds, roughly chopped

Small bunch of fresh parsley, roughly chopped

Small bunch of fresh tarragon, roughly chopped

JUST AS NONNA'S PEAS (page 85) are a go-to at any time of the year, this dish really is best enjoyed in those fleeting weeks of spring, when sweet garden peas—the kind that you buy in the pod and lovingly shell at home—are in season and readily available. The particularly delicate combination of tarragon and parsley does rely on the sweetness of spring peas to enhance the flavor. If you absolutely can't find fresh garden peas in the pod, you could substitute frozen peas, but make sure to buy the small, sweet variety.

Fill a saucepan with cold water, add a teaspoon of salt, and bring to a boil over moderate heat. Add the peas and cook for 5 minutes. Drain well, then put the peas into a salad serving bowl. Season with the olive oil and a little salt while the peas are still warm so they absorb all the flavor, and let cool.

Add the almonds, parsley, and tarragon, then toss everything together well before serving.

ROASTED PUMPKIN WITH ONIONS, RAISINS, AND PINE NUTS

ZUCCA IN SAOR

SERVES 4

1 (2¼-pound / 1kg) pumpkin or butternut squash

6 tablespoons / 100ml olive oil

2 medium onions, halved and thinly sliced

A generous pinch of salt

⅓ cup / 50g raisins

1 teaspoon black peppercorns

3 dried bay leaves

½ cup / 100ml apple cider vinegar

¼ cup / 60ml dry white wine

¼ cup / 25g pine nuts

TO COOK *IN SAOR* IS THE VENETIAN WAY. It's a dialect expression that means to cook "with flavor." Practically speaking, this means a sauce of sweet onion, raisins, peppercorns, pine nuts, bay leaves, and vinegar, a combination that sits somewhere between the exotic and the deeply comforting. Venetians mostly use this sauce when cooking fish—sardines, scampi, or sole, for example, might be dusted in flour, pan-fried, and served in saor. But here I've added it to roasted pumpkin (though roasted butternut squash works equally well); the buttery flesh, slightly burnt and caramelized, pairs beautifully with the sweet and sharp flavors of the sauce. The dish keeps well, as the flavors only improve as they have time to develop. Eat warm or cold, with bread or polenta, or as a side to meat or fish alike.

Preheat the oven to 400°F.

Halve the pumpkin, scoop out and discard the seeds, then slice into half-moon wedges, roughly 2 inches long; leave the peel on. You can cut this into pretty much whatever shape you like, though you want good-sized chunks so they hold their shape when cooked. Arrange the pumpkin in a lightly oiled roasting pan and roast for 25 to 30 minutes, until tender when pierced with a fork. When the pumpkin is cooked, remove the pan from the oven and let cool until you can just handle it.

Meanwhile, pour the olive oil into a large frying pan and set on medium heat. Add the onions and the salt. Cook, stirring, until the onions begin to soften and turn translucent, 5 to 10 minutes. Add the raisins, peppercorns, and bay leaves, and give everything a good stir. Cover the pan and cook until the ingredients are well softened, 20 minutes. Pour in the vinegar and the wine, and simmer until the sauce reduces a little, 8 to 10 minutes. Add the pine nuts and stir well.

Very gently separate the pumpkin flesh from the peel and discard the peel. Arrange half the pumpkin wedges on a large serving dish, then cover with half the sauce. Top with the rest of the pumpkin, and then the remaining sauce.

SLOW-COOKED PEPPERS

PEPERONATA ALLA
VENEZIANA

SERVES 4 TO 6

¼ cup (½ stick) / 50g salted butter,
at room temperature

3 tablespoons / 50ml olive oil

4 anchovy fillets, roughly chopped

6 bell peppers, cored and
roughly chopped

2 firm medium tomatoes, peeled
and chopped

THERE IS AN ITALIAN SAYING, *"fare la scarpetta,"* the meaning of which gets rather lost in translation, but in English equates literally to "do the little shoe." It's what you say when you mop up the very last of the juices on your plate with a chunk of bread. It is a universal sign of a good meal greedily enjoyed, and there is no dish, in my mind, so perfectly suited to *fare la scarpetta* as this *peperonata.* I would go so far as to say that the red, buttery juices are the best bit.

I like to use a mix of red, orange, and yellow bell peppers, partly because I enjoy the colors, but also because I find them to be sweeter than the green variety. And for those who don't like anchovies, do not be put off by them here, nor be tempted to leave them out. The flavor melts away into the butter—you would never even know they were there, except for the hint of delectable creamy saltiness they leave behind. Feel free to make this in advance if you like, as the *peperonata* will keep in the refrigerator for a good few days.

Also, if you fancy something a little more lavish, try scattering a few flaked almonds or roughly chopped hazelnuts over the peppers.

In a small bowl, use a fork to mix the butter and olive oil to a thick paste. If the butter is still a bit cold, you may find that it forms little lumps; don't worry too much about this, as it will all melt into a nice sauce once it is heated in the pan. Lightly whisk the anchovies into the butter and oil.

Spoon the anchovy mixture into a large, heavy-bottomed saucepan set over medium heat. Add the peppers and tomatoes. Stir well with a wooden spoon and let cook until the peppers start to shrink a little and the chopped tomatoes have melted into the sauce, 5 to 10 minutes. Cover the pan, lower the heat to medium-low, and simmer until the peppers become caramelized, soft, and wilted, 35 to 45 minutes. Every now and then, lift the lid, take a look at the peppers, and give them a good stir with the wooden spoon. The longer you cook the peppers, the more tender and sweeter they become.

Serve either hot or at room temperature. (The peppers will keep in an airtight container in the fridge for 2 to 3 days.)

ZUCCHINI, BACON, AND PECORINO TART

TORTA SALATA CON ZUCCHINE, PANCETTA, E PECORINO

SERVES 6

1 block (14-ounce package) /
1 (395g) package prepared puff
pastry, thawed if frozen

4 medium or 3 large zucchini
(roughly 1¼ pounds / 600g)

1 tablespoon olive oil

A generous pinch of salt

½ cup / 70g cubed pancetta

3 large eggs

¾ cup / 180ml heavy cream

⅔ cup / 60g grated pecorino cheese

5 to 6 zucchini (squash)
flowers (optional)

PUFF PASTRY, FRESH ZUCCHINI, AND SALTY PANCETTA is a combination that is almost impossible to resist. This recipe is inspired by a pie served at Trattoria alle Vignole, one of my favorite *trattorie* in Venice, which runs as a restaurant in the summer months and holds the inimitable charm of also being a family kitchen. So whenever I bake this, I can't help but think of lazy summer lunches there, sitting at the picnic bench under the big shady tree where we always look out on the lagoon, glittering hypnotically in the bright midday sunshine.

I sometimes add a few saffron-hued zucchini flowers on top, mostly because I think they look beautiful, though they are by no means essential.

Preheat the oven to 400°F. Grease a 9-inch (23cm) tart pan with a little butter or oil, then dust it with flour until well coated.

Roll out the puff pastry into a large circle and drape it over a 9-inch (23cm) tart pan. Press the pastry into the nooks and crannies, then roll a rolling pin over the top to cut away the excess pastry. Cover the pastry with a sheet of parchment paper and fill it with baking beans or weights. Set the pan in the oven and bake for 15 minutes, until dry to the touch. Remove from the oven, discard the baking paper and beans, and bake for 3 to 5 minutes more to crisp up the base.

Meanwhile, roughly slice the zucchini into rounds 1 inch (2 to 3cm) thick. Drizzle the olive oil into a large saucepan, set on medium heat, and add the zucchini and salt. Cook, stirring, until the zucchini begin to color very lightly, 3 to 5 minutes. Toss in the pancetta and cook, stirring, until the pancetta is crisp, 3 to 5 minutes more.

In a large bowl, whisk the eggs and cream with a fork, then whisk in the cheese. Season with a little salt. Allow the pancetta and zucchini mixture to cool a little (so that it doesn't cook the eggs), then add it to the eggs and cheese, and toss well.

Pour the filling into the prepared pastry shell. If using, open the zucchini flowers very gently and pull out and discard the stamens. Then arrange the flowers on the top of the pie, gently pressing them into the filling. Bake the pie for 20 to 25 minutes, until golden on top. It's delicious eaten warm from the oven or at room temperature.

ROASTED RADICCHIO WITH POMEGRANATE

RADICCHIO ALLA GRIGLIA
CON MELOGRANO

SERVES 6

3 heads of Tardivo radicchio

¼ cup / 60ml olive oil

1 teaspoon Maldon or kosher salt

Freshly ground black pepper

½ pomegranate

RADICCHIO IS A KIND OF CHICORY that is local to the Veneto region. It comes in many different shapes and sizes, and the kind here, known as Tardivo, has long spindly leaves (not unlike the tentacles of an octopus) and hails from the town of Treviso. It's milder and slightly sweeter tasting than most of the other varieties of radicchio.

I eat this dish rather like a warm salad in the winter. The shades of red—the deep burgundy of the radicchio and the shimmering ruby of the pomegranate seeds—are a welcome burst of color on the plate during those austere months. The sprinkling of sharp, sweet pomegranate seeds against the charred, bitter radicchio is by no means conventional, but the combination works just beautifully, especially when seasoned generously with olive oil and salt. If you can't get hold of Tardivo radicchio, which can sometimes be tricky to source outside of Italy, then red chicory works well instead. It has a slightly different texture but a lovely, bitter flavor.

Preheat the oven to 350°F.

Quarter the heads of radicchio lengthwise and arrange the wedges in a large baking dish. Drizzle with the olive oil and season generously with the salt and pepper.

Roast for 15 to 20 minutes, until the tips of the radicchio leaves begin to curl and crisp up; if you plunge a knife into the body of the radicchio, it should feel tender. Transfer the radicchio to a serving platter.

Scoop the seeds of the pomegranate out of their shell (see page 191) and sprinkle generously over the cooked radicchio, then drizzle with a little more olive oil, if you like. Serve while still warm.

ARTICHOKE PUFF PASTRY PIE

TORTA SALATA DI CARCIOFI

SERVES 6

1 (17-ounce) package / 2 (320g) packages prepared puff pastry, thawed if frozen

2 medium potatoes (about 12 ounces / 300g), roughly chopped

6 baby artichokes

2 tablespoons olive oil

1 medium onion, roughly chopped

A generous pinch of salt

1 cup / 100g grated hard cheese, either Parmesan or pecorino

3 large eggs

Freshly ground black pepper

THE INSPIRATION FOR THIS RECIPE IS a particular artichoke pie that is sold by the slice in one of my favorite bakeries in Venice. Made with puff pastry, it is so light and buttery I will happily walk across town just for a slice. I bake the pie in a 9-inch (23cm) cake pan rather than in a pie plate or tart pan, as I like a homemade pie to look homemade. There is a certain rustic charm about it.

This is one of those dishes that works just as well for a fancier dinner party as for a weeknight supper or summer picnic. Serve this with a peppery green rocket (arugula) salad, and you need little else.

Preheat the oven to 400°F.

On a cool, clean surface, unfold and shape one sheet of the puff pastry to fit into the bottom and a bit up the sides of a 9-inch (23 cm) round cake pan, preferably springform. Prick the pastry with a fork, and line it with parchment paper and baking beans or weights.

Bake the pastry shell for 15 minutes, until dry to the touch. Remove the beans and paper, as well as the side of the springform, and cut around the top of the pastry, leaving sides at least 1½ inches (4cm) high. Bake for 2 to 3 minutes more to crisp the pastry shell. Remove from the oven and let the pastry cool.

Fill a medium saucepan with cold water and add the potatoes. Set the pot over medium heat and bring to a boil, then simmer until the potatoes feel tender when you poke a fork into them, 15 to 20 minutes. When the potatoes are done, drain in a colander, then chop into small chunks.

Cut the stems off the artichokes, and peel away and discard any tougher outer leaves until you get to the tender center. Thinly slice the artichoke halves lengthwise into strips.

Drizzle the olive oil into a large frying pan set over medium heat and add the onion and a pinch of salt. Cook, stirring, until the onion begins to turn translucent, 3 to 5 minutes. Add the sliced artichokes, give everything a good stir, and cook until the slivers of artichoke begin to brown very slightly, about 10 minutes.

Remove the pan from the heat and stir in the grated cheese. Crack 2 of the eggs into a large bowl and lightly beat with a fork, then toss into

the artichoke mixture. Add the potatoes to the pan and stir well. Season with salt and pepper to taste.

Spoon the filling into the pastry shell and use the back of a spoon to spread it evenly. Gently unfold and lower the second sheet of puff pastry over the top of the pie and use a pair of scissors to trim away any excess pastry. Use moistened fingers to seal the edges, then use a sharp knife to make 4 slits in the center of the pie to allow the steam to escape. In a small bowl, use a fork to beat the remaining egg, then use a pastry brush to glaze the top of the pie.

Bake for 25 to 30 minutes, until golden brown on top. Serve warm or at room temperature.

WHITE ASPARAGUS WITH ZABAIONE SAUCE

ASPARAGI BIANCHI CON ZABAIONE

SERVES 4

A generous pinch of salt

16 thick white or green asparagus spears, trimmed

Olive oil, for drizzling

4 large egg yolks

½ cup / 120ml Prosecco or other sparkling white wine

1 tablespoon sugar

TO MAKE THE ZABAIONE SAUCE, you whip egg yolks with Prosecco (or, in some cases, Marsala) over very gentle heat until you have a sauce that is light and frothy as air. Zabaione is usually made with sugar and served as a dessert; here, though, I have made something that loosely resembles a hollandaise sauce, but because it is made without butter, it is lighter to eat and somewhat simpler to make.

White asparagus is famously grown in the Veneto region and Bassano del Grappa, which is about an hour's drive from Venice. Legend has it that in the sixteenth century, Bassano was hit by a hailstorm that destroyed most of the harvest. Desperate for food, the farmers dug underground in search of roots and discovered an asparagus that was white in color (due to the lack of sunlight) and very delicate in flavor. Now white asparagus is regularly cultivated underground or blanched (covered) to hide it from the sun.

Use a potato peeler to cut away any parts that look woody—run the blade from the top of the asparagus, just under its bud, all the way down to the bottom. Then take a sharp knife and carve the bottom of the asparagus into a point. This last step isn't necessary, but is a habit I picked up from my mother, who prepares asparagus that way. I think it adds a rather elegant touch to an otherwise simple dish. This zabaione sauce also works well when served with a good-quality jarred variety of white asparagus.

Bring a large pan of salted water to a gentle boil over moderate heat. Tie the asparagus into bundles using kitchen twine, and cook them standing upright until tender, 12 to 15 minutes. (The cooking time will vary depending on the thickness; keep testing by lifting one out and gently prodding it with a knife.) Drain well in a colander, remove the twine, and arrange on a platter. Drizzle the warm asparagus with a little olive oil and set to one side to eat warm or at room temperature. (You can make these ahead of time, if you like, and store covered in the refrigerator for a few hours. Bring to room temperature before serving.)

Fill a saucepan up to one-third with cold water and bring to a boil over moderate heat. Combine the egg yolks, wine, sugar, and a pinch of salt in a heatproof bowl that fits snugly over the saucepan; be careful that the hot water doesn't touch the bottom of the bowl, as that will cause the eggs to scramble. As the water begins to boil, beat the mixture with a handheld mixer until the sauce thickens, is light and frothy, and doubles in volume, 3 to 5 minutes.

Drizzle the sauce generously over the asparagus and sprinkle liberally with salt, then serve immediately.

SPINACH, RICOTTA, AND MINT PIE

TORTA SALATA DI SPINACI, RICOTTA, E MENTA

SERVES 6 TO 8

1 (14-ounce) package / 2 (320g) packages rollable pie crust dough, thawed if frozen

———

1 pound / 500g frozen chopped spinach

———

1 tablespoon olive oil

———

1 cup / 250g ricotta

———

¼ cup / 20g grated Parmesan cheese

———

3 large eggs

———

A generous pinch of salt

———

Freshly ground black pepper

———

Small bunch of fresh mint, leaves finely chopped

———

THIS IS ONE OF THE FEW OCCASIONS when I prefer to cook with frozen produce rather than fresh. I do this partly for the sheer convenience of being able to improvise this dish at the last minute, but largely because when laced with so much cheese and flavorful herbs, frozen spinach works just fine. In fact, it works so much so that I often serve the pie filling without its pastry, as a kind of creamed spinach dish—mix the Parmesan, ricotta, and mint into the wilted greens as per the recipe, omit the egg, and serve warm.

If, however, you prefer to make this pie with fresh spinach, you will need roughly 2¼ pounds (1kg); it shrinks a lot when cooked. Just wash the leaves under cold running water, cut away and discard the large stalks, and wilt in a large saucepan for 10 to 15 minutes.

The trick when making this pie is to squeeze out all excess water from the spinach. This will prevent the flavors from being watered down, and it will also ensure that the pastry crisps nicely. To do this, either press the spinach into a sieve or, if you don't mind getting your hands dirty, squeeze the greens in your hands until no more liquid comes out.

———

Preheat the oven to 400°F.

On a cool, clean surface, roll out the 2 sheets of pie crust dough and use a sharp knife to cut 2 large circles: one will be a slightly larger base for the pie, big enough to drape over sides of the pie plate while allowing for a roughly ¾-inch (2cm) overhang; and a smaller one for the top, just large enough to seal the pie. Gently lay a 9-inch (23cm) pie plate over the sheets and use it as a guide to cut your circles. Cover and set aside the small circle and any remaining trimmings.

Drape the larger circle over the pie plate, then very gently press it into the pan. If you need to, use the trimmings to patch any holes. Line the crust with parchment paper, fill with baking beans or weights, and bake for 15 minutes, until dry to the touch.

Remove the crust from the oven, remove the beans and paper, and bake for a further 2 to 3 minutes until lightly colored. Let cool for a few minutes.

Meanwhile, defrost the spinach. Place the frozen spinach in a large frying pan with the olive oil, and set it over medium heat to warm through, 3 to 5 minutes. (Alternatively, use a microwave to thaw the spinach following package instructions, then drizzle with the oil for added flavor.)

recipe continues

Put the thawed spinach in a medium bowl, taking care to squeeze out all the excess water. Add the ricotta, Parmesan, and 2 of the eggs, then stir well. Season with salt and pepper to taste. Stir in the mint, and then spoon the filling into the pastry case, spreading it out evenly.

Gently lift the second circle of pastry, lay it over the top of the pie, and seal the edges. Roll out the scraps and cut into leaf shapes to decorate the pie, if you wish. Use a sharp knife to make 4 slits at the center of the pie to allow steam to escape. Crack the remaining egg into a small bowl, and beat vigorously with a fork, then use a pastry brush to glaze the pie.

Set the pie in the oven and bake for 30 minutes, until golden brown and warmed all the way through. If you need to check, slide a knife into one of the slashes right down to the middle of the pie; it should come out feeling warm to touch.

Remove the pie from the oven and let cool for 5 to 10 minutes. Then slice and serve warm or at room temperature.

A TAVOLA

CLASSIC LUNCH
RECIPES

ONE OF THE THINGS THAT I find most comforting about Venice is the gentle sounds that come with day-to-day life, somehow more noticeable here than in other cities, perhaps because they're not drowned out by the hum of cars. To most people, these sounds are perhaps unremarkable; but for me they're laced with nostalgia, in that same way that if you grow up by a railroad you might find the rumbling of the trains comforting. There are the church bells that boom on the hour every hour, setting the pace so deftly that you find yourself relying upon them to tell the time. The boats reversing through the canal behind our house—the gentle purring of the motor in the water and the gruff voice of the driver, always in dialect, as he negotiates the tight corners. The sounds from people's homes that reverberate out into the street, because windows are more often than not left wide open, and old walls, it seems, carry noise. Someone talking loudly, perhaps, the radio playing, or that unmistakable tinny click-clacking of plates being stacked and the sounds of knives and forks as they scrape on china. That, I think, is my favorite sound of all. The sound of lunch.

"*A tavola*" is the call to lunch. The interruption of daily business in the middle of the day to make time for a good meal is as punctual as the bells chiming for one o'clock, and it sweeps across the city like a thick, muffling blanket. The city center, where the crowds are, still bustles, unperturbed. The restaurants, of course, remain open. But the residential quarters of town, the back streets, the alleyways with the funny names, the ones that seem to lead nowhere—there, all businesses close, schools end, shops shut. And with the very fewest of exceptions, everyone makes his or her way home to eat with the family. It's as if the city holds its breath—no sound except that delightful chorus of a meal being enjoyed that floats out through open windows and the thin cracks in the ramshackle shutters.

What follows here is a collection of recipes that I cook time and time again for my family and friends, more often than not for lunch, though there is no reason why they shouldn't be enjoyed for dinner, too. They are mostly recipes that can be thrown together quickly, but still feel like a proper meal. Though there are a few dishes, like the ravioli (page 141) and the *pasticcio* (page 147), which call for a slightly greater investment of time, most of the dishes are variations on the theme of pasta, risotto, and polenta—the staples of Venetian home cooking. And there are a few simple, one-pan meat-based dishes thrown in for good measure too.

Broadly, these are all recipes you can easily scale to cook for twelve, dress up fancy and serve on nice platters for a dinner party, or cook for two and share, by the forkful, from the saucepan (if you must). Pasta, rice, and polenta, in particular, are pantry ingredients, readily available in most supermarkets, yet they boast the magical property of being consistent crowd-pleasers. They are starters, main courses, sides, and whole meals; they are what you want them to be.

I do sometimes make fresh pasta. I do so because it is a fun thing to do, because I enjoy the feel of the dough in my hands, and because kneading, rolling, and making shapes is a lovely way to pass the afternoon, often with my little boy—better still that we can then all sit down to eat what we have crafted together. But I do not subscribe to the view that pasta need be either fresh or homemade to be worthy of serving to guests. What in Italy we call *pasta asciutta*, dry pasta, of a good brand made of durum wheat semolina, is all you need, and all you could want for. The magic of a good bowl of pasta, you see, lies in the detail of how it is cooked, rather than how the pasta is made. It is how much salt you add to the water (always so much more than you think it should be; Anna Del Conte says 2 teaspoons per liter [4½ cups] of cooking water); whether you check that it is cooked al dente, when it still has bite to it; the way you scoop a cup of cooking water from the boiling pot, then add it to the sauce to give it that more-ish salty creaminess, which pasta in Italy always has a way of having.

I must admit, I don't always find time to pause for lunch these days—at least not properly, for the three-course meal of *primo*, *secondo*, and *dolce* as other Venetians do. But even if I don't observe the lunch hour as strictly as I might, I value its spirit in the way I cook. We always do our best to eat together as a family—that, at least, is set in stone. And because ritual is everything when it comes to food, I take as much care laying the table whether we're sitting down to a plate of scrambled eggs on toast or to a celebratory feast. I do this because I enjoy it: food tastes better when you eat it from a nice china plate, with a proper knife and fork, and with a cheery bunch of flowers to decorate the table.

LINGUINE WITH ASPARAGUS AND PROSECCO

LINGUINE CON ASPARAGI
E PROSECCO

SERVES 4

1 tablespoon olive oil

1 small onion, chopped

Maldon or kosher salt

14 ounces / 400g thin green
asparagus (about 18 spears),
trimmed and cut into pieces
1 to 2 inches (3 to 5cm) long

5 tablespoons / 100ml Prosecco
or other white sparkling wine

Freshly ground black pepper

A handful of fresh flat-leaf parsley,
leaves roughly chopped

1 pound / 400g linguine or tagliolini

2 tablespoons / 30g butter

⅓ cup / 30g grated
Parmesan cheese

COOKING WITH PROSECCO ALWAYS SEEMS rather extravagant, but less so if you take it as an excuse to enjoy the rest of the bottle with the meal. Inevitably that is what we do. You could, of course, make this using a dry white wine or a splash of vermouth, but there is something about the delicacy of the sparkling wine that works particularly well here. This is a light and airy dish, and you can almost taste the bubbles in the sauce. If you can use a fresh egg pasta, even better still.

Drizzle the olive oil into a large frying pan set over medium heat. Add the onion and a generous pinch of salt, and cook, stirring, until the onion becomes translucent, 5 to 10 minutes.

Add the asparagus and Prosecco, then season with salt and pepper to taste. Reduce the heat to medium-low and cook, stirring, until all the wine has evaporated and the asparagus are cooked (you should be able to pierce them with a paring knife and feel little or no resistance), roughly 5 minutes. If the asparagus are not quite done by the time the wine evaporates, then add a little water to the pan, just enough to cover the bottom, and keep cooking the asparagus until done. Stir in the chopped parsley.

Fill a large saucepan with water and salt it generously. Set the pan on high heat and bring to a boil. Add the pasta and cook as per the instructions on the package. Just before you drain the pasta, scoop ½ cup of the salted cooking water out of the pot and set to one side. Drain the pasta, return it to the saucepan, and add the reserved cooking water, little by little, and the butter. Stir well, then add the asparagus mixture. Give everything one last good stir, and top with the grated Parmesan cheese before serving.

BIGOLI WITH CREAMY WALNUT SAUCE

BIGOLI IN SALSA DI NOCI

SERVES 4

1½ cups / 160g walnut pieces

⅔ cup / 30g stale bread cubes

⅔ cup / 160ml whole milk

⅓ cup / 30g grated Parmesan cheese, plus more for serving

2 tablespoons / 20g pine nuts

1 small garlic clove

5 tablespoons / 70ml olive oil

⅔ cup / 160ml heavy cream

A generous pinch of salt

1 pound / 400g bigoli pasta or spaghetti

BIGOLI IS A KIND OF VENETIAN PASTA that is made by extruding a whole wheat dough through a machine. They are big fat noodles, rather like spaghetti but with a rougher surface texture that allows the pasta to soak up even more sauce. If you visit Venice, you must try fresh bigoli.

Pasta is a comparatively new addition to the Venetian diet. When the pastas from Southern Italy, like maccheroni and spaghetti (made by extruding wheat dough, as opposed to cutting it like ravioli or rolling it like gnocchi), became fashionable in the nineteenth century, the Veneto answered with bigoli. Initially they made them with what they had to hand: buckwheat or whole wheat flour and duck eggs (growers kept—and still do keep—ducks in the marshes around the lagoon). A special die and a quirky-looking piece of kitchen equipment, called a *bigolaro*, were devised to extrude this harder whole wheat dough, which tends to stick in traditional pasta machines.

Two classics are *bigoli in salsa*, an anchovy sauce for which you can find a rough recipe in the sidebar on page 17, and *bigoli con arna lessà*, a ragù made with the heart, liver, and gizzard of a duck (the rest of the bird is usually served later as the main course). A *salsa di noci* is not traditional with bigoli, but its milder flavor and creaminess is a very nice complement to the nutty whole wheat pasta. You can buy dried bigoli in most Italian delicatessens, or you can substitute dried whole wheat spaghetti, fresh spaghetti, or pici.

Fill a large saucepan with water, set it on high heat, and bring to a boil. When the water begins to boil vigorously, toss in the walnuts and boil for 5 minutes to loosen the skins. Drain and lay the walnuts on a clean tea towel. Rub them roughly with the cloth to get most of their skins off, let them dry a little, and leave to cool.

Place the bread cubes in a small bowl. Pour the milk over the bread and let steep for a few minutes, until it has soaked up all the liquid.

Put the bread, its milky juices, the walnuts, Parmesan, pine nuts, and the garlic in a food processor. Pulse for a few minutes, then slowly pour in the olive oil and cream. Process until you have a creamy sauce. Season with salt. (The sauce will keep in an airtight container in the fridge for 5 days.)

Fill a large saucepan with water and salt it generously. Set it on high heat and bring to a boil. Add the pasta and cook al dente as per the instructions on the package.

recipe continues

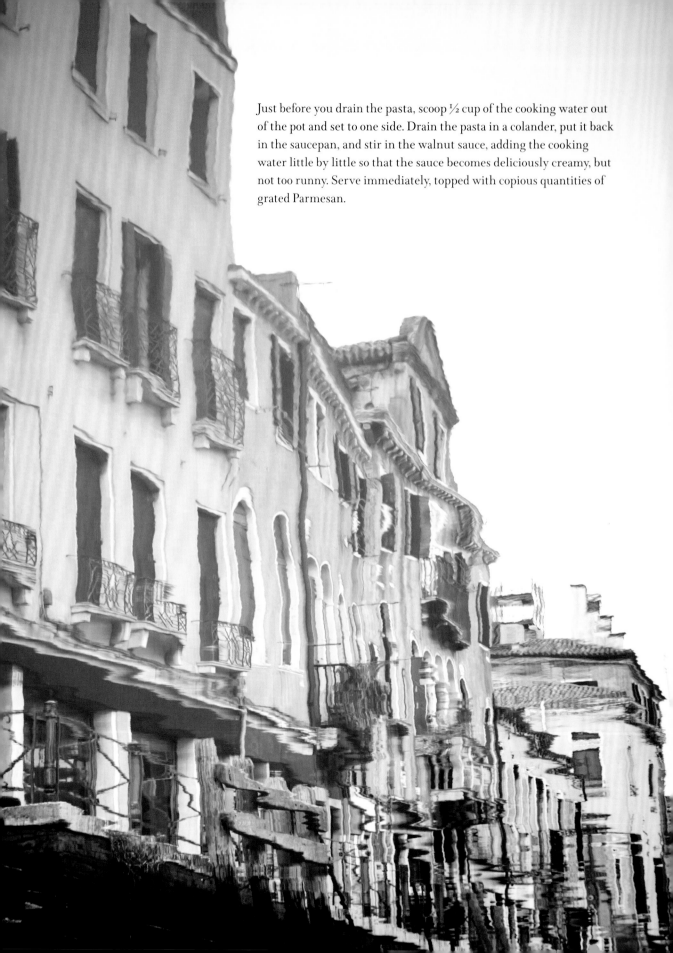

Just before you drain the pasta, scoop ½ cup of the cooking water out of the pot and set to one side. Drain the pasta in a colander, put it back in the saucepan, and stir in the walnut sauce, adding the cooking water little by little so that the sauce becomes deliciously creamy, but not too runny. Serve immediately, topped with copious quantities of grated Parmesan.

TAGLIOLINI WITH SHRIMP, ZUCCHINI, AND SAFFRON

TAGLIOLINI CON SCAMPI, ZUCCHINE, E ZAFFERANO

SERVES 4

½ teaspoon saffron threads

Salt

2 tablespoons olive oil

1 small onion, finely chopped

2 medium zucchini, roughly chopped

10 ounces / 300g jumbo shrimp or prawns, peeled and deveined

3 tablespoons / 50ml dry white wine

⅓ cup / 100ml light cream

14 ounces / 400g tagliolini

TAGLIOLINI ARE ESSENTIALLY VERY FINELY CUT TAGLIATELLE, about as thick as a needle. It is a delicate pasta that complements the simple, fresh flavors of this sauce particularly well. Because tagliolini are so fine, take extra care with their cooking time as, more often than not, I find they're done before I know it. As with the asparagus linguine on page 121, use a fresh egg pasta if you can.

Use a pestle and mortar to grind the saffron strands and a small pinch of salt into a fine powder.

Drizzle the olive oil into a large frying pan set over medium-low heat. Add the onion and a generous pinch of salt, and cook, stirring, until the onion becomes translucent, 5 to 10 minutes. Add the zucchini and cook, stirring, until they begin to color, 3 to 5 minutes. Add the shrimp and wine and cook, stirring, until the wine has largely evaporated and the shrimp have started to turn pink, 2 to 3 minutes. When all the wine has evaporated, add the saffron. Stir well, pour in the cream, and remove the pan from the heat. Season with a little salt to taste.

Fill a large saucepan with water and salt it generously. Set the pan on a high heat and bring to a boil. Add the tagliolini and cook al dente as per the instructions on the package. Just before you drain the pasta, scoop ½ cup of the cooking water out of the pot and set to one side. Drain the pasta in a colander, return it to the saucepan, and add the saffron sauce and—little by little—the reserved cooking water. Toss well and eat immediately, while still warm.

CHICKEN BROTH WITH TORTELLINI

TORTELLINI IN BRODO

SERVES 4

1 medium onion, roughly chopped

2 medium carrots, roughly chopped

2 celery stalks, roughly chopped

1 teaspoon whole peppercorns

Small bunch of fresh parsley

Small bunch of fresh thyme

4 dried bay leaves

Parmesan rind (optional)

3 to 4 chicken wings

3 to 4 pork ribs

1 medium potato, peeled

14 ounces / 400g fresh tortellini

2 tablespoons grated
Parmesan cheese

TORTELLINI IN BRODO IS NOT strictly a Venetian dish: it comes from Bologna. But I remember my mother cooking it for lunch so often in the winter, and it is a dish so laden with childhood nostalgia that I couldn't neglect giving you my recipe for chicken soup with tortellini. I can't tell you how comforting this is to eat.

Anna, a dear friend of mine, makes her own tortellini to cook in broth. Instead of filling the pasta with the traditional mix of prosciutto and Parmesan, she ties them into little knots with no filling at all; she wants nothing to distract from the pure simplicity of the broth. All of this is to say *tortellini in brodo* is more about the soup than it is about the pasta. This meat broth is made with a mix of pork and chicken still on the bone, so it is rich and flavorsome. If I have a leftover Parmesan rind, I throw that in, too. And yet, unlike Anna, I enjoy tortellini that are bursting with cheese and ham floating on top of my broth, and I have absolutely no qualms in buying them ready-made from the shops.

In a large saucepan, combine the onion, carrots, celery, peppercorns, parsley, thyme, bay leaves, Parmesan rind if using, chicken and pork, and 8 cups (1.8L) water. Add the potato whole; it will absorb some of the excess fat from the meat. Set the pan over high heat and bring to a boil. Cover the pot, lower the heat, and simmer gently for 1½ hours, or longer if you like. The longer it simmers, the more flavorsome the broth will become, though don't cook it for much more than 2 to 3 hours.

Remove the pot from the heat and let the broth cool to room temperature. Remove all the large solids from the soup, then pass the liquid through a sieve or cheesecloth once or twice, until you have a clear broth. (The broth will keep in an airtight container in the refrigerator for 2 days.)

When you are ready to cook your tortellini, pour the broth into a large saucepan, set the pan on medium heat, and bring to a boil. Add the tortellini and cook in the broth until they float to the surface, 2 to 3 minutes.

Ladle the soup into individual serving bowls, making sure each gets plenty of tortellini. Sprinkle the grated Parmesan over the broth and serve straightaway.

SPAGHETTI WITH LOBSTER

SPAGHETTI ALL'ASTICE

SERVES 4

1 cooked lobster
(about 1¼ pounds /560g)

2 tablespoons olive oil

1 small onion, chopped

1 cup / 200ml dry white wine

1½ cups / 300ml tomato passata

½ bouillon cube for vegetable
or fish broth

1¼ pounds / 500g cherry tomatoes
(about 40), halved

Salt

Freshly ground black pepper

12 ounces / 350g spaghetti

¼ cup / 50g salted butter

A handful of fresh flat-leaf parsley,
leaves roughly chopped

THIS IS BEYOND A SHADOW OF A DOUBT what I would choose to eat for my last supper, followed by my mother's flourless Chocolate Birthday Cake (page 277). I cannot think of a greater bliss than the mess of spaghetti, tomato, and lobster that is this dish.

The key to making this well is to use juicy, ripe tomatoes and plenty of butter, and to top everything with what looks like far too much parsley. It makes a generous plate of pasta, laced with tomato sauce, the subtle flavor of sweet lobster, and a few chunks of juicy flesh thrown in. If you want to eat more lobster with your pasta, there is nothing to stop you from adding a second one to the pan.

I've made this both with lobster that I bought still living from the fishmonger as well as with lobster that was already cooked. Both work equally well, but because I never enjoy killing a lobster, the recipe I have given here calls for the cooked variety.

Halve the lobster lengthwise with a large knife, from head to tail. Remove and discard the tomalley and coral. Set the lobster aside.

In a large, heavy-bottomed frying pan heat the oil over medium heat, then add the onion. Cook, stirring, until the onion becomes translucent, 5 to 10 minutes. Pour in the wine and the tomato passata, crumble the bouillon cube over the sauce, and give everything a good stir with a wooden spoon. Add the tomatoes and cook, stirring occasionally, for 10 minutes. Now crack the lobster claws and add the claws and tail face side down. Cook for 5 minutes more. Season with a generous pinch of salt and pepper.

Meanwhile, fill a large saucepan with water and salt it generously. Set the pan on high heat and bring to a boil. Add the spaghetti and cook al dente as per the instructions on the package. Just before you drain the pasta, scoop ½ cup of the cooking water out of the pot and set to one side. Drain the pasta in a colander, return it to the saucepan, and add the butter. Stir until the butter melts.

Gently lift the lobster pieces out of the pan and set them to one side. Add the pasta to the frying pan and toss it in the tomato sauce, adding the reserved cooking water little by little. Add about half the parsley to the pan, and toss well. Spoon the pasta onto a serving dish, gently arrange the lobster pieces on top, sprinkle with the rest of the parsley, and serve while piping hot.

HOMEMADE GNOCCHI WITH BUTTER AND SAGE

GNOCCHI FATTI IN CASA
CON BURRO E SALVIA

SERVES 6

FOR THE GNOCCHI

4 medium to large baking potatoes
(about 2¼ pounds / 1kg)

2¾ cups / 350g Italian type "00"
flour or all-purpose flour, plus
more for dusting

2 large eggs

¼ teaspoon ground nutmeg

1 teaspoon salt, plus more for boiling

FOR THE SAUCE

½ cup (1 stick) / 110g salted butter

¼ cup / 60ml olive oil

15 sprigs of fresh sage

Plenty of grated Parmesan cheese,
for serving

ONCE YOU HAVE MADE YOUR OWN GNOCCHI, you will most likely never buy them from a shop again. They are pleasingly simple to make, and whereas pasta dough calls for heavy kneading (which can at times feel a little too much like work), all you do with gnocchi is bring the dry and wet ingredients together with your hands, then roll out the dough. The result pairs just as well with a rich meaty sauce as with a drizzle of oil and a few fresh herbs. They are a delectable meal in themselves.

The secret to good gnocchi is to work the dough while the potatoes are still hot. You press the potato flesh through what in Italy we call a *passaverdura*; in English, that equates to a potato ricer—a peculiar utensil that you will find in every good Italian cook's kitchen. To my shame, I don't own one; when I make gnocchi, I mash the potato flesh through a coarse sieve and that seems to work just fine. Most traditional recipes suggest that you peel and boil the potatoes before mashing them with flour and eggs, but I prefer to bake them. Baking is less labor-intensive, and I find it easier to quickly scoop out the cooked potato, leaving the baked skin, than to peel and chop them before boiling. But better still, I find that drier potatoes give the gnocchi a lighter, fluffier texture.

The ratio of flour to potato depends largely on how wet the potato is. The quantity here is a guide, but feel free to add more or less flour to get the dough to the point where it feels soft but not too sticky to touch. Trust your own instincts and bear in mind that the less flour you add, the lighter the gnocchi will be; I begin with roughly 2 cups (250g) and keep adding little by little, as I need to.

Preheat the oven to 425°F.

Make the gnocchi. Prick the potatoes several times with a fork, then put them on a baking sheet. Bake for 1½ hours, until soft. (Alternatively, cook the potatoes in a microwave on high for 5 to 7 minutes or until soft).

Pour 2 cups (250g) of the flour onto a clean kitchen surface and form a well in the center. Halve the potatoes, scoop out their flesh, discard their skins, and pass the flesh through a sieve or ricer into the well in the flour. Use your hands to create a little hollow in the potato as well, crack the eggs into the hollow, and add the nutmeg and salt. Use your hands to mix everything together, bringing the flour in from the perimeter, until you have a smooth, soft dough. Slowly add the rest of the flour if you need to. You don't want to knead the dough, you just want to bring it together; in fact, the more you work it, the tougher the gnocchi will become.

recipe continues

Divide the dough into 8 to 10 equal chunks. Use the palms of your hands to roll the chunks into balls, and then roll the balls into long ropes roughly ¼ inch (1cm) thick. Cut the gnocchi into pieces that are roughly 1 inch (3cm) long. It is important that the gnocchi are all evenly sized, if not shaped, as their cooking time will vary depending on their size and you want them to cook at the same rate.

Line a baking sheet with parchment paper, dust it lightly with flour, and lay out your gnocchi. Use the back of a fork to press down on each one to create little indentations in their shape. Then roll them over and repeat the process on the other side.

Fill a large saucepan with water, generously salt the water, and bring it to a boil.

Make the sauce. Set a large frying pan on medium-low heat, and add the butter, olive oil, and sage.

Working in batches, add the gnocchi to the boiling water and cook until they float to the surface, 1 to 2 minutes. Use a slotted spoon to fish them out and toss them into the pan with the bubbling butter. Continue to cook the gnocchi.

Cook the gnocchi in the pan just long enough to coat them with the sauce, 1 to 2 minutes. Remove to serving plates while you finish cooking the rest of the gnocchi. Top each serving with copious quantities of grated Parmesan and serve.

GNOCCHI WITH CHERRY TOMATOES AND CRAB

GNOCCHI CON GRANSEOLA E POMODORO

SERVES 6

3 tablespoons / 50ml olive oil

2 garlic cloves, peeled and lightly crushed

1½ pints / 300g cherry tomatoes (roughly 30), halved

¾ cup / 150ml dry white wine

¾ teaspoon red pepper flakes

A medium bunch of fresh parsley, leaves chopped

2 tablespoons / 30g salted butter

Salt

1¼ pounds / 600g gnocchi (page 133 for homemade)

¾ pound / 300g lump crabmeat

6 tablespoons / 30g grated Parmesan cheese

I COULD HAPPILY EAT THIS for lunch every day, forever after. And while gnocchi is not a dish I much think to indulge in during the hot summer months, this is such a heavenly combination of fresh and light flavors that it is a pleasure to eat all year round. I only insist that you heap your plate high with fresh parsley and grated Parmesan before tucking in.

Heat the oil in a large frying pan over medium-low heat. Add the garlic and cook, stirring, until it begins to turn golden, 2 to 3 minutes. Discard the garlic. Add the tomatoes, wine, red pepper flakes, and half the parsley. Simmer on a medium heat until the wine has evaporated and the tomatoes have softened, 7 to 10 minutes. Stir in the butter.

Fill a large saucepan with water, salt it generously, and bring it to a boil. Working in batches, add the gnocchi and cook until they float to the surface, 1 to 2 minutes. Use a slotted spoon to fish them out of the cooking water and toss them in the pan with the tomato sauce.

Take the pan off the heat, add the crabmeat, and give everything a good stir so the gnocchi are coated in the sauce. Top with the remaining parsley and the grated Parmesan, and serve immediately.

THREE KINDS OF RAVIOLI

TRE RAVIOLI

SERVES 4

Homemade pasta is something for special occasions, or for those days when it feels like you have all the time in the world. It is no "better" than dried pasta, just different–a different mood for a different day. And that mood is one that I tend to associate with cozy Sundays. Ravioli are mostly about the filling. And here I have given a pasta recipe with three of my favorites. You will need a pasta machine, though it needn't be either a fancy or expensive gadget. I use the same stainless steel machine with a handcrank that I've had for years.

3 cups plus 3 tablespoons /
400g Italian type "00" flour
or all-purpose flour, plus more
for dusting

———

5 large eggs

———

Filling and sauce of choice
(recipes follow)

———

A generous pinch of salt

———

Olive oil or melted butter (optional),
for serving

———

Pour the flour onto a clean work surface. Pile it up high like a volcano, then make a crater in the center, and crack 4 of the eggs into it. Use your fingertips to break up the yolks and mix the eggs, little by little, into the flour until you have a rough, floury dough. Knead the dough vigorously for about 10 minutes, until it begins to feel lovely and smooth in your hands. The key to making good pasta is to knead the dough well, which allows the gluten in the flour to develop so that the pasta will hold its shape nicely and stay al dente when cooked (otherwise it will turn to mush). Roll the dough into a ball, wrap it in plastic wrap, and set it to rest in the fridge for at least 30 minutes.

Make your filling (recipes follow).

On a generously floured surface, roll out the pasta dough using a rolling pin until it is thin enough to fit into the pasta machine. Roll the dough through each setting on the machine until it's the thinnest it can be. Do this in batches, if easier.

Crack the last egg into a small bowl and beat lightly with a fork. Cut the pasta sheet into 2 equal pieces. On one sheet, spoon 1 teaspoon of filling every 3 to 4 inches (8 to 10cm), then use a pastry brush to paint around each mound of filling with the egg wash. Drape the second sheet of pasta over the first one, like a blanket. Then gently press down around each mound with your fingers to seal the ravioli, taking care to press out any air bubbles, as they will cause the pasta to burst when it cooks. Trim each ravioli with a sharp knife or a ravioli cutter, then gently transfer them to a lightly floured baking sheet. When you have made all the ravioli, cover the sheet with plastic wrap and refrigerate until you are ready to cook the pasta.

Fill a large saucepan with water, salt it generously, and bring it to a boil. Drop the ravioli into the water a few at a time, stir gently, and wait for them to float to the surface, 1 to 2 minutes. Use a slotted spoon to fish the ravioli pieces out into a bowl and transfer them to serving dishes while you cook the remaining ravioli. Drizzle with olive oil or melted butter, if desired.

MASCARPONE, RICOTTA, AND SPECK FILLING

MASCARPONE, RICOTTA, E SPECK

⅓ cup / 100g mascarpone

½ cup / 100g ricotta

10 ounces / 300g speck,
cut into small pieces

¾ cup / 50g dried bread crumbs

A generous pinch of salt

Freshly ground black pepper

SPECK HAILS FROM THE SÜDTIROL REGION, but it is a much-loved staple in Venice, too. You will see it often paired with radicchio (the two go particularly well together), as well as in baked pastas or meat dishes, or, my particular favorite, on pizza. Speck is very similar to prosciutto, but it is lightly smoked and cured with a mix of juniper berries, pepper, bay leaves, and other spices. It works well in filled pasta, especially here, paired with creamy cheese. You should be able to find speck in most Italian delicatessens, but if you can't get hold of it easily, substitute prosciutto crudo. Serve these ravioli with either the melted butter and sage sauce mentioned on page 133 or with a drizzle of olive oil and some freshly ground black pepper.

Spoon the mascarpone, ricotta, speck, and bread crumbs into a food processor, then pulse until you have a thick paste. Season with salt and pepper to taste.

RICOTTA AND LEMON FILLING

RICOTTA E LIMONE

1½ cups / 400g ricotta

Grated zest of 3 small lemons

3 tablespoons grated Parmesan
cheese, plus more for serving

A generous pinch of salt

JUST AS THE PUMPKIN RAVIOLI (see page 000) are rich and hearty—the kind of food you crave in the cold weather—you can taste the freshness of spring in every bite of these. The ricotta filling is creamy and delicate, and should not be marred by a rich sauce. Drizzle the ravioli with a little oil and sprinkle generously with grated Parmesan before you eat, but add nothing more.

Spoon the ricotta into a sieve over the sink and drain any excess liquid for 5 minutes. Pour the ricotta into a small bowl, add the lemon zest, Parmesan, and salt, then lightly beat with a fork until smooth and well combined.

PUMPKIN AND AMARETTI FILLING

ZUCCA E AMARETTI

FOR THE FILLING

3½ cups / 800g cubed pumpkin

2 tablespoons olive oil

1 cup / 100g grated
Parmesan cheese

1 tablespoon apple chutney

⅔ cup / 50g crumbled crunchy
amaretti cookies (9 to 10 large)

Salt

Freshly ground black pepper

FOR THE SAUCE

½ cup (1 stick) / 110g salted butter

¼ cup / 60ml olive oil

About 10 sprigs of fresh sage

A MIX OF PUMPKIN AND AMARETTI, halfway between sweet and savory, this filling is exquisite. Ravioli made with it are best served with nothing more than a drizzle of olive oil or melted butter with fresh sage (see recipe on page 133). Anything more would be too much and would take away from the pasta itself.

Preheat the oven to 425°F.

Make the filling. Spread the pumpkin on a baking sheet, and drizzle with the olive oil. Roast for 30 to 40 minutes, until the pumpkin is tender. A paring knife inserted into a chunk should meet no resistance. Let the pumpkin cool for 10 minutes, then peel away and discard the skin.

Mash the pumpkin flesh into a smooth, creamy puree. Spoon the puree onto a clean tea towel, tie it loosely in a bundle, and squeeze tightly to remove excess water. If the pasta filling is too watery, the ravioli won't hold their shape when they cook.

Put the pumpkin puree into a large bowl and stir in the grated Parmesan, chutney, and crumbled cookies. Season to taste with salt and pepper.

Make the sauce. Heat the butter, olive oil, and sage leaves in a large frying pan over medium heat, and cook until the butter is melted and the leaves are slightly crisped.

PHEASANT AND RADICCHIO LASAGNA

PASTICCIO DI FAGIANO E RADICCHIO

SERVES 6

1 cup / 250ml vegetable broth

½ cup / 120ml olive oil, plus more for drizzling on top

2 (1½-pound) / 2 (800g) pheasants, rinsed

⅔ cup / 90g cubed pancetta

2 shallots, chopped

2 garlic cloves, chopped

3 dried bay leaves

½ cup / 130ml dry white wine

A generous pinch of salt

Freshly ground black pepper

3 heads of radicchio, a mix of Treviso for the sauce and Tardivo for decoration

10 ounces / 300g fresh lasagna noodles

2¾ cups / 700g crème fraîche

1 cup / 90g grated Parmesan cheese

PASTICCIO IS WHAT IN VENICE we call a baked pasta, but it is also an expression that you use when something is a "sticky mess." Pasticcio's "messiness" is wonderfully liberating for the cook: not only is it okay for the sheets of pasta not to be perfectly lined up and for the melted cheese to be spilling over the top of the dish—but in fact, that is how it should be.

The secret to a really good *pasticcio* lies in the flavor of the meat sauce. That is where you will invest most of your time and reap the highest rewards. Here I have made a ragù of pheasant, to which I've added a little pan-fried radicchio and layered it with cheese and pasta before baking it in the oven. (You can make the ragù ahead of time and then either store the sauce in an airtight container in the fridge for a couple of days or freeze it for a few months.)

Most baked pasta recipes call for a béchamel sauce, which I find rather heavy. Instead, I've layered the meat and pasta with crème fraîche and grated Parmesan, which make the dish lighter. If you want a richer flavor still, try substituting mascarpone for the crème fraîche.

In a small saucepan set over medium heat, bring the vegetable broth to a boil.

Meanwhile, add 4 tablespoons (60ml) of the olive oil to a heavy-bottomed casserole or Dutch oven set over medium heat and arrange the whole pheasants in the pot. Cook, turning the birds now and then, until they are lightly browned all over, 4 to 7 minutes. Remove the birds from the pot, then add the pancetta and cook, stirring frequently, until colored, 3 to 5 minutes. Add the shallots, garlic, and bay leaves and cook, stirring, until the shallots color a little, 5 minutes. Add the wine, let it bubble for a minute or two, then pour in the boiling broth. Season with salt and pepper, and bring to a simmer. Return the pheasants, fit a lid snugly on the pot, and cook gently until the meat is falling off the bone, 1 hour.

Lift the pheasants onto a carving board. Discard the bay leaves. Let the birds cool a little, then pull the meat off the bone and shred it. Put the pot back over low heat, and stir the shredded meat into the cooking juices. If the sauce is too soupy, increase the heat to medium and cook until reduced to the consistency of gravy.

In a medium frying pan set on medium heat, drizzle in 2 tablespoons of the olive oil. Roughly chop 2 radicchio into small pieces, and toss in the pan along with a generous pinch of salt. Cook until the leaves begin to

recipe continues

color and tenderize, 3 to 5 minutes. Spoon the cooked radicchio into the pot with the pheasant and stir well to mix all the flavors.

Preheat the oven to 375°F.

Cut the remaining radicchio lengthwise into slices roughly 1 to 2 inches (3 to 5 cm) thick. Drizzle the remaining 2 tablespoons olive oil into a large frying pan, arrange the slices of radicchio in a single layer in the pan, taking care they don't overlap, sprinkle generously with salt, and cook until lightly colored and the leaves become tender, about 5 minutes. Remove the pan from the heat.

Spread one-third of the ragù in the bottom of a large, deep baking pan about 10 by 12 inches (25 by 30cm). Cover with a single layer of lasagna noodles, spread one-third of the crème fraîche evenly over the noodles, and sprinkle one-third of the grated Parmesan over the top. Repeat this layering two more times. Arrange the slices of grilled radicchio on top of the lasagna and drizzle with a little olive oil.

Cover the dish with foil and bake for 20 minutes. Remove the foil and continue baking until deliciously golden and bubbly on top, 30 more minutes.

BAKED POLENTA WITH MELTED GORGONZOLA

POLENTA PASTICCIATA
CON GORGONZOLA

SERVES 4

8 cups / roughly 1.4kg
cooked polenta

3 cups / 200g crumbled
gorgonzola cheese

½ cup / 50g grated Parmesan
cheese

1 cup / 60g coarse bread crumbs

3 tablespoons / 40 g
salted butter

THIS DISH IS DESIGNED TO MAKE USE of leftover polenta by layering it with melted gorgonzola and grated Parmesan, then baking it in the oven until irresistibly golden. It has come to be such a favorite of mine that I find myself cooking polenta with the express purpose of then making a pasticciata. With a little crisp green salad on the side, it is a meal in itself.

For this, I use instant polenta. Whereas normal polenta requires 40 minutes or so of standing over the pot and stirring, instant polenta is, much as its name suggests, both quick and easy to cook. To make the polenta, follow the instructions on the box, but essentially you bring a generously salted pot of water to a boil, then sprinkle in the polenta, little by little, stirring all the while until you have a thick, bubbly yellow cream. When you add the polenta, you should pour it in *a pioggia* ("like a rainfall")—this will stop it clumping together and becoming lumpy. Pour it into a dish and leave it to cool and set, which takes 10 to 15 minutes. You can also make the polenta a couple of days ahead and then keep it in the fridge, but I rarely find myself able to resist it that long.

Preheat the oven to 350°F.

Cut the polenta into rounds (about 2 to 3 inches [6 to 8cm] in diameter; I usually use a cookie cutter to do this, though the exact size and shape matters little) and arrange a layer of polenta rounds in the bottom of a baking dish.

Dot half of the polenta here and there with the gorgonzola. Arrange a second layer of polenta slices over the gorgonzola and top with what is left of the cheese. Sprinkle with the Parmesan and bread crumbs, and dab the butter here and there over the top.

Bake for 15 to 20 minutes, until all the cheese is golden brown and melted on top.

ARTICHOKE, FAVA BEAN, FARRO, AND MINT SALAD

INSALATA DI CARCIOFI, FAVE, FARRO, E MENTA

SERVES 4, WITH LEFTOVERS

1 cup / 200g pearled farro

8 to 10 baby artichokes

Zest and juice of 1 lemon

3 tablespoons / 50ml olive oil, plus more for drizzling over the salad

½ cup / 120ml dry white wine

3 cups / 450g shelled small fava beans (if larger, they will need to be peeled)

A generous pinch of salt

Freshly ground black pepper

Small bunch of fresh parsley, leaves chopped

Small bunch of fresh mint, leaves chopped

4 ounces / 120g ricotta salata

VENICE SITS RIGHT ON THE ADRIATIC SEA, and while you might not think of it as a "beach town," the Lido and its long stretch of sandy beach, dotted with old-fashioned parasols and Visconti-esque beach huts, become the center of the city's life during the summer months.

Summer days on the Lido are all about the picnic lunch, which in my mind is forever associated with *insalata di riso*, a simple cold rice salad dressed with some variation of tuna, hard-boiled eggs, olives, grilled vegetables, mozzarella, and any other leftovers you might have sitting around in the kitchen. This recipe is a slightly more sophisticated twist on the summer favorite. I have made it with farro, which I prefer to the more traditional plain white rice: it is nuttier in flavor and has a crunchy texture that lends itself so well to this kind of salad. I've also included crumbled ricotta salata (which is slightly firmer and saltier than plain ricotta), but you could just as well make it with a punchier feta cheese or with a mellow mozzarella—or leave the cheese out altogether. If you can't get your hands on fresh baby artichokes, then feel free to make this using the canned variety; likewise, feel free to use frozen fava beans or even lima beans.

In a large saucepan, cover the farro with a couple inches of water, then set over high heat and bring to a boil. Lower the heat to medium and simmer until the farro is al dente, 20 to 25 minutes. Drain the farro and pour it into a large bowl.

Tear away and discard the tougher outer leaves of the artichokes, and trim the spiky tops. Toss the artichokes into a bowl of cold water with half the lemon juice to stop them from turning brown.

Heat the olive oil in a large frying pan over medium heat. Quarter the artichokes and add them to the pan; give them a good shake, and turn them to coat them well in the oil. Pour in the wine, reduce the heat to low, and cook, stirring occasionally, until the artichokes are tender, about 15 minutes. Add the fava beans and cook, stirring, until they become tender, 5 to 7 more minutes. (To use canned artichokes and fava beans, bring the wine to a boil in the pan and simmer to reduce for a minute before tossing in the beans and simmering for 3 minutes, then add the artichokes along with the olive oil and stir. Cook for another minute so that all the vegetables are tender and heated through.) Season with salt and pepper to taste, then stir in the lemon zest and the remaining lemon juice.

Add the artichokes and fava beans to the farro. Dress the salad with a drizzle of olive oil, and season with salt and pepper to taste. Toss in the parsley and mint, then crumble in the ricotta.

LEMON RISOTTO

RISOTTO AL LIMONE

SERVES 4

2 medium onions

1 medium carrot

1 celery stalk

1 vegetable bouillon cube

2 tablespoons olive oil

A generous pinch of salt

1½ cups / 350g arborio rice

½ cup / 100ml dry white wine

2 lemons

2 tablespoons / 30g salted butter

⅓ cup / 30g grated
Parmesan cheese

WHEN I WAS GROWING UP, we often ate this for lunch at school. My school was a crumbling convent hidden behind the extravagantly baroque church of Santa Maria della Salute. It wasn't in any way a fancy school, but it had the prettiest cloisters in which we played during morning break. Lunch was in a cavernous hall, and I still remember the nuns sweeping out of the kitchen doors at noon, carrying large pots of steaming risotto that they would dish out by the ladleful.

As with all risotto, the secret to success is in the stock. This recipe combines a bouillon cube with boiled carrot, celery, and onion for a vegetable broth that is more flavorful than what you might find in a container, but less time-consuming to make than homemade stock. My friend Maria, who is one of the best cooks I know, taught me this trick.

Take care when cooking the risotto that you not overcook it; or it will become mushy; the rice should have a little bite to it.

Quarter one onion and finely chop the other. Chop the carrot and celery into large chunks.

Fill a medium saucepan with roughly 7 cups (1.7L) water, add the quartered onion, carrot and celery, and bring to a boil over medium heat. Reduce the heat and simmer for 15 minutes or so. Crumble in the bouillon cube.

In another medium saucepan heat the olive oil over medium heat and add the chopped onion and a pinch of salt. Cook, stirring, until the onion becomes soft and translucent, 5 minutes. Add the rice. Increase the heat to high and cook, stirring with a wooden spoon, until you feel the rice starting to stick to the pan and you hear it crackling a little, 2 to 3 minutes. Add the wine and give it all a good stir. Cook, stirring constantly, until all the liquid is absorbed, 3 to 5 minutes. Then lower the heat to medium and begin to add the warm broth, ladle by ladle through a strainer, stirring and waiting until the liquid has been absorbed before adding more. The idea is to keep the consistency of the rice wet and to keep the rice moving by stirring constantly, so that it will cook evenly. Continue in this manner until the risotto is done: the rice should feel plump and tender, but still be firm at its center, 15 to 20 minutes. (You may not need all the broth; just keep adding until the rice is cooked.) Grate the zest of one of the lemons into the pan and squeeze in its juice. Cook, stirring, to allow the flavors to develop, 3 to 5 minutes.

Remove the pan from the heat, let sit for a couple of minutes, then add the butter and stir until it has melted into the rice. Add the Parmesan, stir again, and serve piping hot with additional grated lemon zest on top.

GARDEN PEA AND PANCETTA RISOTTO

RISI E BISI

SERVES 4

6¾ cups/ 1.5L chicken stock

½ cup / 70g cubed pancetta

⅓ cup / 75g salted butter

1 medium onion, finely chopped

A generous pinch of salt

Heaping 1½ cups / 350g vialone nano rice

⅔ cup / 150ml dry white wine

2⅔ cups / 400g shelled garden peas

Freshly ground black pepper

½ cup / 60g grated Parmesan cheese

Small bunch of fresh parsley, leaves chopped

WE CELEBRATE THE DAY OF SAINT MARK, the patron saint of Venice, on April 25, by custom with a plate of risi e bisi. Shelling fresh peas for *risi e bisi* marks the beginning of spring for me, and is an important part of what makes this otherwise simple dish special. It is also a task that I have come to find oddly therapeutic—and that I happily share with the rest of the family. The sweetness and freshness of the peas is what differentiates a good plate of *risi e bisi* from an exquisite one. That said, when peas are not in season or you're pushed for time, you can almost as well make a good "*risi*" using frozen sweet peas. Sometimes good is enough.

Unlike the other risotto dishes in this chapter, if I can I make this with vialone nano rice rather than arborio rice. That is because *risi e bisi* is a unique Venetian dish that sits halfway between a risotto and a soup: it should be liquid and verdant. A rice like vialone nano has a very high starch content and holds its shape well when cooked, which is ideal, but if you can't get your hands on it, use arborio instead and be mindful when cooking of the consistency that you would like.

Bring the chicken stock to a boil in a large saucepan. Cover the pot, reduce the heat to low, and leave it at a simmer.

Set a large saucepan on medium heat, add the pancetta, and cook, stirring, until it begins to color, 3 to 5 minutes. Add half the butter, all of the onion, and a generous pinch of salt. Cook, stirring, until the onion becomes soft and translucent, 5 minutes. Add the rice. Increase the heat to high and cook, stirring with a wooden spoon; you should feel the rice begin to stick to the pan and hear it crackling a little. Add the wine and give it all a good stir. Cook, stirring constantly, until all the liquid is absorbed, 3 to 5 minutes. Add the peas and 2 ladlefuls of stock. Cook, stirring occasionally and waiting until the liquid has been absorbed before adding more stock. Keep your stirring to a minimum, so that the peas are not too squashed. The rice should be cooked after 15 to 20 minutes (it should be creamy and tender but still firm to bite), and the final result should be halfway between a soup and a risotto.

Season with salt and pepper to taste, remove the pan from the heat, add the remaining butter, and stir through until melted. Just before serving, sprinkle each plate with the grated Parmesan and the parsley.

FENNEL RISOTTO

RISOTTO DI FINOCCHIO

SERVES 4

6½ cups / 1½L good-quality
beef stock

½ cup (1 stick) / 100g salted butter

1 medium onion, chopped

1 large fennel bulb, finely sliced

A generous pinch of salt

Heaping 1½ cups / 350g arborio rice

½ cup / 50g grated
Parmesan cheese

RISOTTO IS WHAT MY MOTHER would cook on Sunday nights to banish the blues, and it is what I cook for my own family when we are in need of food that nourishes the soul as much as the body. It is comfort food.

This recipe is adapted from one in Mariù Salvatori de Zuliani's classic Venetian cookbook, *A Tola Co I Nostri Veci*. I fell in love with the delicate flavors and the unexpected twist on an otherwise classic risotto. While risotto recipes tend to be quite formulaic, you will find this one is a little unusual: there is no white wine, just lots of butter, cheese, and stock. And while you might expect to make it with a delicate, vegetable-flavored broth, I prefer a beef stock, which has more flavor. The result is a wonderfully creamy dish, with just a hint of sweetness from the fennel.

As with all risottos, use a good-quality stock—from your butcher or otherwise the very best you can get your hands on. If you are cooking for vegetarians, substitute vegetable broth, and compensate by adding a pinch more salt to taste.

Bring the stock to a boil in a medium saucepan, reduce the heat, and keep at a simmer.

Melt about two-thirds of the butter in a large saucepan set over medium heat. Add the onion, fennel, and a generous pinch of salt. Cook, stirring, until the vegetables become tender and translucent, 5 to 10 minutes. Add the rice. Increase the heat to high and cook, stirring with a wooden spoon, until the rice starts to stick to the pan and is crackling a little, 2 to 3 minutes. Add a ladle of the stock, and give everything a good stir. Cook, stirring constantly, until all the liquid is absorbed. Add the stock ladle by ladle, stirring and waiting until the liquid has been absorbed before adding more. The idea is to keep the rice wet and to keep it moving by stirring constantly, so that it will cook evenly throughout the risotto. Continue in this manner until all the stock has been absorbed into the risotto, and the rice becomes plump and tender, but still firm at its center, 15 to 20 minutes.

Remove the pan from the heat and let sit for 1 to 2 minutes. Then vigorously stir in the remaining butter and the grated Parmesan. This final step is called *mantecare* and is what gives the rice that irresistible creaminess.

RISOTTO WITH RADICCHIO AND GORGONZOLA

RISOTTO CON RADICCHIO E GORGONZOLA

SERVES 4

6 cups / 1.5L good vegetable broth

2 tablespoons olive oil

2 tablespoons / 30g salted butter

1 medium onion, chopped

Salt

3⅓ cups / 200g stemmed and thinly sliced radicchio

Heaping 1½ cups / 350g arborio rice

½ cup / 100ml dry white wine

¼ cup / 90g cubed gorgonzola dolce

½ cup / 100ml light cream

¼ to ½ cup / 20g grated Parmesan cheese

THERE ARE A THOUSAND AND ONE WAYS to cook radicchio, a number of which have made their way into this book. This is perhaps my favorite. The risotto is beautifully creamy, and when you add some of the bitter red leaves to the rice right at the end, they barely cook and stay just a little crunchy—they also give the risotto a wonderfully seductive shade of deep claret.

The three most common varieties of radicchio used for cooking are *radicchio di Chioggia*, which looks rather like a round red cabbage and has a very bitter flavor; *radicchio di Treviso*, which is tall and pointed, looks like a deep red chicory, and has a slightly milder flavor; and *radicchio Tardivo*, so-called because it is a late bloomer, which has a very distinctive form with long spindly, reddish leaves and is the mildest tasting. On balance, *Tardivo* is my preference, as its leaves hold their shape very nicely when cooked, but any variety will do.

Bring the broth to a boil in a medium saucepan, reduce the heat, and keep at a simmer.

Set a large, heavy-bottomed saucepan on medium heat and add the olive oil and butter. As the butter begins to melt, add the onion and a pinch of salt. Cook, stirring, until it begins to soften and turn translucent, 5 minutes. Add half the radicchio and give everything a good stir. Then add the rice. Increase the heat to high and cook, stirring with a wooden spoon, until the rice begins to stick to the pan and you hear it crackling, 3 minutes. Pour in the wine and stir until most of the liquid has evaporated. Add the broth ladle by ladle, stirring and waiting until the liquid has been absorbed before adding more. The idea is to keep the rice wet and keep it moving by stirring constantly, so that it will cook evenly. Continue in this manner until the rice is done: it should be plump and tender, but still firm at its center, 15 to 20 minutes. (Don't feel that you need to add all the stock, just keep adding it to the rice until it is cooked.) A few minutes before the rice is done, stir in the remaining radicchio.

In a small saucepan set over low heat, combine the gorgonzola and cream. Heat until the cheese is melted and you have a creamy sauce, 3 to 4 minutes.

Remove the rice from the heat, cover, and let rest for a couple of minutes, then pour in the melted gorgonzola and cream. Stir well, add the Parmesan, and stir again. Serve piping hot.

CHICKEN IN TOMATO AND WHITE WINE SAUCE

POLLO IN TECIA

SERVES 4

2 tablespoons olive oil

1 small fennel bulb, chopped

1 medium onion, chopped

1 garlic clove, chopped

Salt

4 chicken thighs

4 chicken drumsticks

½ cup / 120ml dry white wine

1 (8-ounce) / 1 (230g) can
diced tomatoes

4 sprigs of rosemary

4 fresh bay leaves

Freshly ground black pepper

CHICKEN IS NOT SOMETHING you will often see on the menu at Venetian restaurants, but chicken cooked this way—what in dialect we call *in tecia* ("in the pot")—is classic Venetian homecooking. Traditionally, this dish is made with a whole chicken chopped into pieces, and there is no reason why you shouldn't make it that way. However, given the choice, I prefer a mix of thighs and drumsticks, which are the most flavorsome parts of the bird, especially when served in the delicious tomatoey sauce.

You must serve this with hot, runny yellow polenta. To make the polenta, bring 4 cups of well-salted water (a generous teaspoon) to a rolling boil in a large saucepan over medium heat. Gradually pour 1 cup of polenta into the boiling water in a steady stream, whisking all the while. Continue whisking until the polenta is thickened, then turn the heat to low, and continue whisking until the polenta has thickened enough that it doesn't settle back to the bottom of the pan when you stop stirring. Cover the pan and cook the polenta for 30 minutes, stirring vigorously every 10 minutes or so to keep it from sticking to the sides and bottom of the pan. Stir in a couple tablespoons of butter and serve immediately.

In a large pan set over low heat, combine the olive oil, fennel, onion, garlic, and a sprinkle of salt. Cook, stirring, until the onion and fennel begin to turn translucent, 5 to 10 minutes. Add the chicken, skin side down, increase the heat to medium, and cook the chicken, turning it every now and then so it browns lightly and evenly on all sides, about 10 minutes.

Pour in the wine and let everything cook until most of the liquid has evaporated, 5 minutes. Add the tomatoes, rosemary, and bay leaves.

Cover the pan, reduce the heat to low, and cook until the chicken is cooked through, 25 minutes. If the sauce is too liquid, remove the lid, increase the heat to medium-high, and cook until the liquid has reduced to the desired thickness. It should be a rich, thick sauce, not soupy. Season with salt and pepper to taste, and serve hot with the polenta.

SLICED VEAL IN CREAMY TUNA AND CAPER SAUCE

VITELLO TONNATO

SERVES 4

2 (4-ounce) / 2 (120g) cans of oil-packed tuna

4 heaping tablespoons good-quality mayonnaise

3 anchovy fillets

4 gherkins, chopped

1 tablespoon drained capers, plus more for garnish

7 to 10 drops of Tabasco sauce, or to taste

10 ounces / 300g cold sliced roast veal (or turkey breast)

THIS IS ONE OF THOSE DISHES that neither sounds nor looks half as good as it tastes, largely because the sauce (made from a heavenly mix of tuna and mayonnaise) is a rather bland beige color. But trust me when I tell you that it is a keeper: a childhood favorite that works just as well for quick kitchen lunches as for fancy dinner parties. In fact, I asked my mother to make this for our wedding party the night before my husband and I married.

This dish is traditionally made with cold roast veal, but you can just as well make it with roasted turkey breast, very thinly sliced, if you prefer. It is a great way to make use of leftover light meat, both veal and turkey: just slice the meat as thin as you can, arrange on a plate, and spoon over the creamy sauce. It's particularly nice served with a salad of Butter Beans with Sage (page 93) or a crisp arugula salad dressed with a little olive oil, lemon juice, and a pinch of salt. Also, bear in mind that any tuna sauce you might have left over is heaven spread on crusty white bread as a sandwich filling.

Drain the oil from the tuna, then spoon the tuna, mayonnaise, anchovies, and gherkins into a blender. Rinse the capers under cold water to rid them of excess salt and add to the blender as well. Blend until smooth, then add the Tabasco sauce and blend until well combined. The sauce is ready as is, or you can pass it through a strainer to make it silky smooth. Refrigerate until you are ready to use.

Arrange the veal on a serving plate, spoon the sauce over, and sprinkle with more capers.

SPICED MEATBALLS

POLPETTINE PICCANTI

**MAKES 32 MEATBALLS,
ENOUGH TO SERVE 4 TO 6**

1½ pounds / 600g ground beef

2 cups / 100g fresh bread crumbs

1 medium onion, chopped

2 peeled garlic cloves, one chopped
and the other left whole

2 sprigs of rosemary,
leaves chopped

¼ teaspoon ground cumin

¼ teaspoon ground coriander

1 large egg

A generous pinch of salt

Freshly ground black pepper

4 tablespoons / 60ml olive oil

3⅓ cups / 750g tomato sauce

¼ teaspoon red pepper flakes

Small bunch of fresh parsley,
leaves chopped

Small bunch of fresh basil,
leaves chopped

IF YOU WALK ACROSS VENICE—all the way from the Castello quarter, where I live—you will end up somewhere near the Jewish quarter, or Ghetto. This area is worth a visit, if only for the fact that it's the first ghetto ever built; indeed, the word itself comes from the Venetian dialect *ghéto*. It is a particularly charming part of town: quiet and peaceful, with kosher butchers, restaurants, and bakeries on every corner, all brimming with exotic delights—one of my favorite places to head to simply for a stroll as well as to soak up the atmosphere, which is quite distinct from that of any other quarter of Venice.

This recipe is loosely adapted from one I came across in a book on traditional Jewish Venetian cookery, and it has come to be a favorite in my kitchen. It is both comforting and wonderfully rich in flavor, owing largely to the mix of cumin, coriander, red pepper flakes, and fresh herbs that season the meatballs. Traditionally you might serve this with hot, runny yellow polenta (see page 162); but when I fancy something a little lighter, I just serve the meatballs as is with a crisp green salad dressed with a drizzle of olive oil, a squeeze of lemon, and a generous pinch of Maldon (or kosher) salt.

In a large bowl, combine the ground meat, bread crumbs, onion, chopped garlic, rosemary, cumin, coriander, egg, and a generous pinch of salt and pepper. Give everything a good stir with a wooden spoon, then use your hands to roll the mixture into small balls roughly the size of a walnut.

In a large frying pan set over medium heat, add 1 tablespoon of the olive oil and the whole clove of garlic. Cook until the garlic begins to brown, 3 minutes. Add the tomato sauce, red pepper flakes, and a little salt and pepper. Reduce the heat to low and keep at a simmer.

In a large frying pan set over high heat, add 3 tablespoon of the olive oil. Working in batches, cook the meatballs, turning them now and again (I find it easiest to do this using two spoons), until they are browned all over, 3 to 5 minutes. Try not to overcrowd the pan. Transfer the cooked meatballs to the pan of tomato sauce as they finish cooking and continue to fry the remaining meatballs.

Simmer the meatballs in the sauce, so they soak up all the delicious flavor, 5 to 10 minutes. Remove the pan from the heat. Generously heap the parsley and basil over the meatballs before serving piping hot.

LO SPRITZ

RECIPES FOR A
VENETIAN APERITIVO

AT THE VERY HEART OF VENETIAN LIFE is the *campo*. The *campo* is kind of a mini *piazza*—less imposing, less fancy, and as commonplace as intersections or crosswalks in other cities. If you have spent any time wandering around Venice, you will know that the town itself is a maze of tiny alleyways, called *calli*, which open onto these *campi*.

Every Venetian grows up and lives out his or her life in the neighborhood *campo*. That's where they play hide-and-seek as children, where they dry their laundry as grown-ups. I live in Campo delle Gorne, and have done so since I moved to Venice when I was six years old. It's not a grand square, not as far as they go. There's a sleepy canal and a few houses with old windows, mostly left open so you can peer into the neighbors' kitchens—which, of course, I love to do. Like most of the squares in Venice, we have a *pozzo*, an ancient well that once upon a time provided drinking water. And we have a tree. The tree is pretty special: not many *campi* have a tree.

Just by the edge of the canal, in the far corner of the *campo*, farthest from our house, is a rickety wooden table with three mismatched chairs. That is where the old men of the *campo* sit, sometimes chatting and often in companionable silence. Their faces are worn and wrinkled, their shorts are always impeccably ironed, and one of them wears a fedora; they are characters that seem to have stepped out of a Fellini movie. Come late afternoon, like clockwork, they gather around the little table with a few rough glass tumblers in hand, a carafe (usually of something sparkling), and sometimes a bowl of potato crisps or a brown paper bag of *pizzette* from the local bakery. Then they sit there for hours, watching the world go by and enjoying what you might call an apéritif, but in Venice we call *lo spritz*.

A spritz, of course, is strictly speaking a drink. Deliciously crimson in color, it is made by mixing part white wine, part Campari (or another bitter—Select or Aperol, say), and part sparkling water—the precise quantities dictated by how you like to drink it. But in Venice, *lo spritz* is so much more than a drink; really, it is a cultural institution. The drink lends its name to that time of the day when, as the sun begins to go down, you meet with friends, open a bottle, eat a few *stuzzicchini*—a bowl of salted almonds or some olives, perhaps a few salty potato crisps, and a couple of *cicheti*, too—"small bites," not so much to fill you up as to tide you over until dinner.

Cicheti are as much an important part of *lo spritz* as the drink itself. And it is by intention that this chapter, while named after a cocktail, includes only a handful of drink recipes. For the rest it is all about the food: the sort of food that you share, a little bite of this and a little bite of that. These are simple dishes, like crostini with creamy burrata or ricotta and a little fruit–whatever is in season or is in the larder: chunks of bread with mortadella or prosciutto; leftover risotto, say, rolled in bread crumbs and deep-fried until decadently crisp and brown; or miniature pizzas made with buttery puff pastry and melted, oozing mozzarella.

By tradition, *cicheti* are eaten out, usually standing at a bar, or what in Venice we call a *bacaro*. It is food that is designed to be social. What I like most, however, is when friends come to us. Sometimes I mix a big carafe of spritz proper, or in summertime, when peaches are in season, I can't resist making everyone a Bellini. Other times, we do little more than open a bottle of Prosecco–that works, too. What I find, though– and this is perhaps the most charming aspect of indulging in *lo spritz* at home–is that more often than not, while friends are invited only for drinks and a few bites, we all eat so much and linger so long that *lo spritz* happily turns into dinner.

ZUCCHINI PIZZETTE

PIZZETTE DI ZUCCHINE

MAKES 8 TO 10 PIZZETTE

1 small zucchini

Maldon or kosher salt

1 sheet (½ a 17-ounce package) /
1 (320g) package prepared puff
pastry, thawed if frozen

1 (14-ounce) / 1 (400g) can peeled
plum tomatoes, drained, chopped,
and drained again

4½ ounces / 125g fresh mozzarella,
drained and chopped

½ cup / 50g grated pecorino cheese

Small bunch of fresh thyme

PIZZETTE WITH A BUTTERY PUFF PASTRY BASE are a "thing" in Venice, and they are beyond delicious. At most bars, in fact, you will find on offer both pizzette, which have a breadier dough base that more closely resembles a traditional pizza, and these, which are made with puff pastry and which I always prefer. So, while you will find that this recipe is wonderfully easy to make, you needn't think of it as a cheat's pizzetta—unless, of course, you count cooking with prepared puff pastry as cheating.

I have topped these with grilled zucchini rounds and fresh thyme, but baby artichokes, black olives and anchovies, and blue cheese are all equally scrumptious alternatives—or leave them plain like a margherita.

Preheat the oven to 425°F. Line a large baking sheet with parchment paper.

Using a mandoline, slice the zucchini into paper-thin rounds and arrange on a skillet or griddle. Season with a little salt. Cook on medium-high heat until charred and blistered on both sides, 3 minutes total.

On a cool, clean surface, unfold and lay out the puff pastry. Use a round biscuit cutter, about 3 inches (7 to 8cm) in diameter, to cut out the bases for individual pizzette. Arrange the pastry rounds on the baking sheet, allowing plenty of space between them. Use a sharp knife to score a circle inside each pastry round, allowing a ¼-inch margin.

Bake the pizzette bases until lightly golden, 10 to 15 minutes. Remove the sheet from the oven and use your fingers to squash down the centers of the pastry if they have puffed up; you want to create a hollow. Spoon a heaping teaspoon of tomato into each hollow.

In a medium bowl, combine the mozzarella and pecorino. Spoon a generous scoop of the cheese over the tomato, enough so that the cheese almost completely hides the tomato. Top with a couple slices of grilled zucchini and a few thyme leaves.

Bake for 20 minutes, until the cheese is deliciously melted and golden, and the pastry is crisp on the bottom. The pizzette are best eaten straight from the oven, when buttery and warm, but they will keep in an airtight container for 2 days. Reheat them in the oven before serving.

POPPYSEED PUFFS

SFOGLIATINE DI SEMI
DI PAPAVERO

MAKES 70 TINY PUFFS

1 sheet (½ a 17-ounce package) /
1 (320g) package prepared puff
pastry, thawed if frozen

1 large egg

2 tablespoons poppy seeds

A very generous pinch of salt

OUR LOCAL CAFÉ, known affectionately in our family as the Orange Café, where we just as often go for an aperitivo in the evening as for a brioche and a cappuccino in the morning, makes these little *sfogliatine* using the scraps of puff pastry left over from other baked goods. They serve them along with a bowl of juicy green olives to nibble on when customers have ordered a spritz. It's such a simple idea, but one that never ceases to hit the spot. I bake these in larger batches, then keep them on hand to serve with drinks before dinner, usually with a large chunk of Parmesan cheese that I plonk casually on a wooden board and leave for everyone to break pieces off as they please—rather as you might with a good cheddar. A small word of warning: as we say in Italy, "*uno tira l'altro*"–or, "one calls for another"; that is, once you start nibbling on these, you really can't stop.

Preheat the oven to 350°F. Line 2 baking sheets with parchment paper.

On a cool, clean surface, unfold and lay out the puff pastry. Lightly beat the egg with a fork, then use a pastry brush to brush it over the top of the pastry. In a small bowl, mix the poppy seeds with the salt, then sprinkle generously all over the pastry.

Use a sharp knife to cut the pastry into little rectangles: these needn't be perfectly equally shaped, but I usually cut ten times lengthwise and seven times across, for 70 small puffs. Gently lift the squares onto the baking sheet. Bake for 10 to 12 minutes, until the pastry is puffed up and golden on top.

WALNUT CROQUETTES

CROCHETTE DI NOCI

MAKES 20 TO 24 SMALL CROCHETTE

Maldon or kosher salt

4 medium to large baking potatoes (roughly 2¼ pounds / 1kg), peeled and quartered

1¾ cups / 200g walnuts

2 large eggs

Freshly ground black pepper

1 cup / 120g all-purpose flour

1¾ cups / 120g dried bread crumbs

Peanut oil, for deep-frying

CROCHETTE OF ALL KINDS—potato, cheese, tuna, veal—are a staple in bacari across Venice. Unlike croquetas, their Spanish counterpart, the filling shouldn't be completely smooth and creamy but layered with depth and texture. Walnut and buttery mashed potato is an unusual flavor combination. Unexpectedly rich and—for lack of a better word—earthy, it washes down particularly well with a glass of Prosecco or a dry spritz. This recipe is loosely adapted from that in Maria Agostini's *La Cucina Popolare Veneto-Ebraica*.

Bring a large pot of salted water to a boil. Add the potatoes and cook until tender but still firm, 10 to 15 minutes. You should be able to stick a paring knife into the potato and feel no resistance.

Meanwhile, process the walnuts in a food processor until roughly ground and the texture resembles coarse sand. (If you don't have a food processor, chop the walnuts by hand.)

Drain the potatoes in a colander, then return them to the pot and mash well. Add 1 egg and the yolk of the second egg (reserving the egg white), then stir in the walnuts. Season with salt and pepper to taste.

In a small bowl, lightly beat the reserved egg white with a fork. Arrange a bowl of the flour and a bowl of the bread crumbs next to the egg wash.

Scoop a little of the potato puree in the palm of your hand and roll it into a small ball roughly the size of a golf ball. Dip the ball into the egg white, then into the flour, and finally into the bread crumbs, making sure to cover the ball well. Toss it gently in the palm of your hand to dust off any excess bread crumbs and put the ball on a plate or on a baking sheet. Repeat with the remaining ingredients, Refrigerate the potato balls for 20 to 30 minutes. Chilling them will ensure that they hold their shape well when you fry them.

Pour peanut oil into a large, deep saucepan, making sure the oil doesn't fill the pot more than halfway. Heat over medium heat until the oil is 325°F to 375°F. To test if the oil is hot enough, drop a cube of bread in; it should sizzle and turn golden in 30 seconds. If it browns quicker or burns, then lower the heat a little. Working in batches, lower the potato balls into the hot oil one by one, taking care not to overcrowd the pot. Deep-fry until golden brown all over, about 4 minutes. Gently lift them out of the oil with a slotted spoon and put them on paper towels to soak up excess oil. Sprinkle with salt and serve while still deliciously warm.

DEEP-FRIED RISOTTO AND MOZZARELLA BALLS

ARANCINI

MAKES 15 SMALL ARANCINI

1 large egg and 1 large egg white
———
3 cups / 600g cold leftover risotto
———
⅔ cup / 80g chopped mozzarella,
in 15 small pieces
———
¾ cup / 100g all-purpose flour
———
1 cup / 70g dried bread crumbs
———
Peanut oil, for deep-frying
———
Maldon or kosher salt,
for sprinkling
———

ARANCINI ARE DEVISED TO MAKE USE of leftover risotto; but these bite-size balls of deep-fried rice, oozing with melted cheese, are such a joy to eat that you will find yourself cooking risotto solely for an excuse to make them. This recipe works particularly well with the Lemon Risotto on page 155.

If you want to make the arancini ahead of time, you can deep-fry the whole batch and store them in an airtight container in the fridge for a couple of days. When you are ready to eat them, take them out of the fridge, bring them to room temperature, and serve as is or, better still, reheat in the oven for 10 to 15 minutes so they are all warm and melted at the center.

Crack the whole egg into the leftover risotto and mix with your hands so that the rice forms a doughy paste.

Set up your production line. Set the mozzarella to one side, pour the egg white into a small bowl, pour the flour onto a plate, and pour the bread crumbs onto a second plate.

Scoop a little of the rice mixture (about the size of a golf ball) into the palm of your hand. Use your fingers to make a little hollow in the middle, and fill it with a piece of mozzarella. Shape the rice around the cheese so you have a sealed ball. Dip the ball into the egg white, then into the flour, and finally into the bread crumbs. Roll it around in the bread crumbs to make sure that it is well covered, then toss it gently in the palm of your hand to dust off any excess bread crumbs. Set aside and repeat with the remaining ingredients.

Pour enough peanut oil into a large, deep pot, making sure the oil doesn't fill it more than halfway. Heat the oil over medium heat until it is 375°F. Test if the oil is hot enough by dropping a cube of bread in it; it should sizzle and turn golden in 30 seconds. Working in batches, lower the rice balls into the pot one by one, taking care not to overcrowd the pot. Fry until they are golden brown all over, about 4 minutes. Gently lift them out of the oil with a slotted spoon and put them on paper towels to soak up excess oil. Sprinkle with salt and serve while still warm.

DEEP-FRIED SAGE LEAVES

FOGLIE DI SALVIA FRITTE

MAKE 20

½ cup / 50g Italian "00" flour
or all-purpose flour

½ cup / 100ml chilled mild
carbonated beer

Peanut oil, for deep-frying

20 large fresh sage leaves

A generous pinch of Maldon
or kosher salt

THESE ARE MOSTLY JUST AN EXCUSE to indulge in a salty, golden batter with a very nice hint of fresh herb at its center; but for all their simplicity, there are few words that can describe quite how delightful these are to eat. The soft green-gray sage leaves look as pretty as a picture on the plate, too.

Sift the flour into a large bowl, then gradually pour in the beer, whisking all the while. Keep whisking until you have a smooth batter.

Pour 2 to 3 inches of peanut oil into a deep, heavy pot, taking care that the oil doesn't fill the pot more than halfway. Heat the oil over medium heat until it is 325° to 375°F. To test if the oil is hot enough, toss a cube of bread into the oil; it should sizzle and turn golden within 30 seconds. If it burns, adjust the temperature accordingly.

Hold a sage leaf by its stem and dip it into the batter. Twist it around in the batter, then hold it over the bowl to eliminate any excess. Gently lower the leaf into the hot oil. Fry a few leaves at a time, taking care not to overcrowd the pot, until the sage turns golden on both sides, 40 seconds to 1 minute. Gently lift the leaves out of the pot and lay them on paper towels to absorb excess oil. Sprinkle generously with salt and serve while still hot.

ZUCCHINI, PECORINO, AND FRESH MINT FRITTATA

FRITTATA DI ZUCCHINE, PECORINO, E MENTA DEL GIARDINO

SERVES 6 TO 8, AS BITES

2 tablespoons olive oil

1 medium onion, sliced

A generous pinch of salt

3 medium zucchini, thinly sliced

8 large eggs

1 cup / 100g grated pecorino cheese

3 sprigs of fresh mint, leaves finely chopped

A FRITTATA IS A VERY DIFFERENT BUSINESS from an omelet, not just because the one is Italian and the other French. The omelet is finer, of course, suited to a quick breakfast or lunch for one. A frittata, on the other hand—wonderfully thick and stuffed with vegetables and melted cheese—is without a doubt food for sharing. I like it best cut into rough chunks and eaten with fingers. Unlike the omelet, which you must eat straight from the pan or it will turn to rubber, a frittata, I find, tastes even better at room temperature than it does hot. All of which makes it ideal for cooking ahead.

The flavors here are my pick for a hot summer's day: zucchini and fresh mint (from the garden). But use the recipe as a blueprint and toss in whatever takes your fancy: broccoli (fry in a pan with a little olive oil for 8 to 10 minutes, until cooked, before adding it to the eggs) with black olives, or perhaps red peppers with a smattering of chèvre and chopped fresh parsley.

Heat the olive oil in a large frying pan set over medium heat. Toss in the onion along with a generous pinch of salt. Cook, stirring, until the onion begins to turn translucent, 5 to 10 minutes. Add the zucchini and cook, stirring, just long enough for them to color a little, 3 to 5 minutes. Remove the pan from the heat.

In a large bowl, lightly beat the eggs, and stir in the grated cheese and mint. Pour the cooked vegetables from the pan into the bowl, stir well, season with a little more salt if you like, and then pour the frittata mixture back into the pan. Set over medium-low heat and cook until golden on the bottom, 5 to 7 minutes. Flip the frittata over; I find it easiest to do this by turning the frittata out onto a plate, then gently nudging it back into the pan. Cover the pan and cook until golden on the second side and cooked through, about 5 minutes. Slice and serve while still warm or at room temperature.

BOILED EGGS AND ANCHOVIES

UOVA E ACCIUGHE

SERVES 6 TO 8

4 large eggs

8 anchovy fillets

1 tablespoon olive oil

Freshly ground black pepper

SALTY ANCHOVIES DRAPED OVER HALF AN EGG: this is one of life's great flavor combinations. This is a go-to recipe when guests appear unexpectedly, as we always have eggs in the fridge and a jar of anchovies in the cupboard. The assembling of the two is so mindless that it is very easy to go about it while holding a conversation; in fact, it's so simple that I wouldn't even call it a recipe.

Place the eggs in a saucepan and cover with cold water. Bring to a rolling boil over medium-high heat. Cover the saucepan and take it off the heat. Let sit for 10 minutes. Set a timer; if you leave the eggs longer, the yolks will harden and become less creamy. Drain the water from the saucepan and fill it with very cold water. Let the eggs sit in the cold water until they are cool to the touch, about 1 minute.

Peel the eggs and slice them in half from head to toe. Arrange the egg halves on a serving plate or tray. Drape one anchovy fillet over each egg half, then drizzle with a little olive oil and sprinkle with pepper before serving.

TOASTED HAM AND CHEESE SANDWICH

IL TOAST

MAKES 5 SANDWICHES

8 ounces / 220g Taleggio cheese

1 large egg yolk

1 teaspoon Dijon mustard

1 teaspoon dried sage

Salt

10 thin slices of white sandwich bread

4 ounces / 110g sliced prosciutto cotto

2 tablespoons olive oil

"UN TOAST" IS WHAT IN ITALY we call a grilled ham and cheese sandwich. The best in Venice is without doubt the one they make at Harry's Bar, where the toasts come sliced into neat rectangular pieces, half-wrapped in an elegant white napkin, and served along with Bellinis and Martinis (the first also a Harry's Bar specialty). It is from their cookbook that I have adapted this recipe. Instead of toasting the sandwiches as is most common to do, they deep-fry them in olive oil, a couple of minutes on each side, until the bread is crisp and golden, and the cheese is oozy and irresistibly melted inside.

I have used taleggio cheese here, which is my favorite cheese for melting. It has a smooth texture and a strong flavor without tasting overpowering. The original Harry's Bar recipe and the toast you will find in most cafés in Venice use Swiss, Gruyère, or Emmentaler. I've also added a teaspoon of dried sage to the filling, which is by no means conventional, but prosciutto and sage go so well together that it seems a shame not to.

Put the cheese, egg yolk, mustard, and sage in a food processor, and blend until you have a smooth, spreadable sauce. (If need be, thin the paste with a dash of cream.) Taste and season with a little salt, bearing in mind that the prosciutto will be quite salty.

Cut the crusts away from the bread, then spread the cheese mixture on one side of all the slices. Arrange the prosciutto over the cheese and top with a second slice of bread. Press the sandwiches firmly together.

Pour the olive oil into a large frying pan, and heat over medium-high heat until the oil becomes very hot. Add as many sandwiches as will fit comfortably in the pan; if need be, cook them in batches. Fry the sandwiches on one side for no more than a couple of minutes, until the bread turns golden brown. When you see the edges of the sandwich begin to color, turn them over and fry on the second side.

Cut the sandwiches in half and eat straightaway.

THREE KINDS OF CROSTINI

TRE CROSTINI

Crostini are nothing more than rough slices of crusty bread, usually baguette, topped with whatever you fancy. They're probably the most popular kind of cicheti, and you will see them piled high on the countertop at every Venetian bacaro. This is not really a matter of cooking—more just simple assembling of a few choice ingredients. Here are a few of my favorite flavor combinations.

CROSTINI WITH BURRATA AND POMEGRANATE

CROSTINI CON BURRATA E MELOGRANO

SERVES 4 TO 6

1 small loaf of crusty white bread, such as baguette or ciabatta

1 burrata cheese

1 pomegranate

1 tablespoon olive oil

A generous pinch of Maldon or kosher salt

THIS IS ONE OF THOSE RARE DISHES that looks every bit as beautiful as it tastes. Creamy, snow-white burrata, slathered on bread and topped with pomegranate seeds that shimmer like precious gems: it's truly a feast for the eyes. Don't forget to drizzle the crostini generously with olive oil and salt before serving, as that really brings the flavors together.

Cut the bread into thick, rough slices. Tear open the burrata and spoon the creamy middle onto the bread.

Roughly roll the pomegranate around on a hard surface to loosen its seeds. Score around the middle of the fruit with a sharp knife, then tear it open with your hands. Hold one half over a bowl and tap forcefully with a wooden spoon, squeezing a little to remove the seeds. Use a teaspoon, if need be, to scoop the rest of the seeds out. Repeat with the remaining half.

Sprinkle the ruby-red seeds over the cheese, drizzle with a little olive oil, and sprinkle with a pinch of salt.

CROSTINI WITH MORTADELLA AND PISTACHIOS

CROSTINI CON MORTADELLA E PISTACCHIO

SERVES 4 TO 6

1 small loaf of crusty white bread, such as baguette or ciabatta

4 ounces / 120g thinly sliced mortadella

A handful of pistachio nuts, roughly chopped

IN ITALY YOU WILL FIND THAT MORTADELLA often comes already peppered with chunks of lemony green pistachios: the two go very well together. My suggestion here is to pile the meat on the bread and top it with crushed nuts—not quite so sophisticated, perhaps, but every bit as delectable.

Cut the bread into thick, rough chunks. Arrange a couple slices of mortadella on the bread, then sprinkle the pistachios over the meat.

CROSTINI WITH RICOTTA, HONEY, AND FIGS

CROSTINI CON FICHI, RICOTTA, E MIELE

SERVES 4 TO 6

1 small loaf of crusty white bread, such as baguette or ciabatta

½ cup / 125g ricotta

8 fresh figs, halved

2 tablespoons good-quality thin honey

A generous pinch of Maldon or kosher salt

THIS IS A FAVORITE FLAVOR COMBINATION OF MINE: evidence that sometimes the very best food involves no cooking at all. The dish relies on the figs being plump, the cheese fresh and creamy. A delicious alternative to making crostini is to omit the bread, lay out whole ricotta on a generous serving dish, strew the cheese with a few fresh figs roughly torn open to reveal their voluptuous centers, and drizzle with a little honey. Therein you have the beginnings of a sumptuous meal.

Cut the bread into thick, rough slices and top with a generous chunk of ricotta. Arrange the figs over the cheese. You can stem and peel the figs if you prefer, though I am rather partial to the rich hues and texture of the skins, so I don't usually bother. Drizzle liberally with the honey and sprinkle with salt just before serving.

LAYERED GORGONZOLA, PEAR, MASCARPONE, AND WALNUT LOG

TORTINO DI GORGONZOLA, PERA, MASCARPONE, E NOCI

SERVES 6

12 ounces / 350g gorgonzola dolce

1 pear, cored and thinly sliced

½ cup / 150g ricotta

½ cup / 150g mascarpone

A handful of walnut halves

1 loaf of bread, such as ciabatta or baguette

THIS RECIPE CAME ABOUT BY HAPPY ACCIDENT while I was scrambling to toss together some sort of food for friends who joined us unexpectedly for a spritz. Like many of the other *cicheti* in this chapter, this concoction can't really be described as cooking; it's merely the assembling of a few ingredients that happen to go very well together. There is no prescriptive way of serving this, but I like to lay the *tortino* on a board with a loaf of bread on the side, so that everyone can help themselves by smearing the fruit and cheese onto the bread as they so choose.

The log should keep for an hour or two when stored in the fridge, though be wary of preparing it too far in advance, as the pears will brown with time. I think crisp pears are best for this, as their crunchy texture counterbalances the soft cheese, but that is purely a matter of taste. I have used gorgonzola dolce here, which is milder and a little creamier than its more mature counterpart, gorgonzola piccante. If you can't find gorgonzola, then substitute Dolcelatte or another blue cheese of your choosing.

Lay the gorgonzola on a wooden board or serving plate. I like to spread it out in a rectangular shape—the exact dimensions matter little, but you want a thick layer of cheese. Arrange half the pear slices over the gorgonzola, then spread the ricotta over the pear. Now, arrange the rest of the pear slices over the ricotta. Spread the mascarpone over the pear, and top with the walnut pieces. Serve with the bread on the side.

THREE
PROSECCO
COCKTAILS

TRE APERITIVI COL
PROSECCO

Prosecco is the drink of choice in Venice, be it mixed with a scarlet bitter, fresh fruit juice, or by itself. These are some of my favorite variations for an aperitivo.

SPRITZ

THE SPRITZ IS UBIQUITOUS IN VENICE. Legend has it that it was introduced by the Austrians, during their occupation of the city in the late nineteenth century. It has many incarnations, mixed with all manner of bitters, of which Campari and Aperol are possibly the most famous, and Cynar—a curious dark bitter made from the petals of artichokes—the most exotic. Every barman will have his own ratio for making a spritz, just as every Venetian will have his or her own preferred way of drinking it. Feel free to play around with the quantities and proportions here, and adjust to your taste. Three constants, however, which remain nonnegotiable are: ice, an olive, and a slice of citrus.

Fill a glass with ice cubes, and pour in one part Prosecco, one part bitter—your choice, be it Campari, Aperol, or Cynar—and one part soda water. Garnish with a briny olive and a slice of orange.

BELLINI

COCKTAILS HAVE A QUASI-MAGICAL WAY OF lending old-world, white-glove glamor to even the grayest and most mundane of days. Bellinis, if for no other reason than their extravagantly pink color, particularly induce this effect.

The secret to a really good Bellini lies in the quality of the peaches you use to make the juice. Harry's Bar, where the cocktail was created, famously mixes the drink with juice from a can, but I infinitely prefer a Bellini made with beauteous, fresh sweet fruit. This comes with the caveat that, unless you freeze peach puree in bulk (which can, of course, be done), you will only be able to make Bellini in the summertime. But I think that only adds to the romance of it. It goes without saying that if you can't find white peaches, you can use yellow ones—though the Bellini, of course, won't be pink.

Peel and halve 3 or 4 white peaches, which should be enough to make a generous jug of the cocktail. Scoop out and discard the stones, then roughly chop the fruit and toss it in a blender to puree until smooth. Refrigerate until cold. Mix one part fresh peach puree to three parts chilled Prosecco.

ROSSINI

THE ROSSINI IS THE LESSER KNOWN but no less delightful cousin of the Bellini. Three parts chilled Prosecco to one part fresh strawberry puree, and named after the early-nineteenth-century opera composer Gioachino Rossini, it is wondrously delicious. To me, a bright red jug of Rossini speaks of sunny crisp spring afternoons, just as a jug of peachy Bellini speaks of balmy hot summer evenings.

Hull and roughly chop 1 quart / 500g fresh (or frozen) strawberries, which should be enough to make a generous jug of the cocktail. Toss the fruit in a blender with a squeeze of lemon and a teaspoon or two of sugar, then puree until smooth. Refrigerate until cold. Mix one part fresh strawberry puree to three parts chilled Prosecco.

LA LAGUNA

FISH AND GAME FROM
THE VENETIAN LAGOON

LOOK AT A MAP OF VENICE, and you will see a shape rather like a fish: a gathering of tiny islands, threaded together by bridges and canals. Look again at the map, this time more closely, and you will notice a number of small, individual islands dotted here and there around the city. These specks and splotches, some bigger and some smaller, seemingly inconsequential and easily overlooked, appear rather like satellites floating around the heart of the city. Yet for Venetians, these islands—and the way of life there, still largely unaffected by the tourist trade—are much of what it means to really be Venetian.

Each island boasts its own character, industry, and way of life. On Burano, the island with the rainbow-colored houses, they weave lace by hand and make buttery *buranelli* cookies in the shape of an S; on Murano, they blow glass so fine and delicate it's famous far and wide; on Torcello, where Hemingway once lived and where today there is a population of eleven people, they grow the very finest artichokes. There are countless other islands, of course, some of which I know well, like Sant'Erasmo, where the bulk of Venice's fruit, wine, and vegetables come from; or Pelestrina, where the larger share of Venice's fishermen live, work, and trade. Others—many, in fact—I don't even know the name of, though we have sped past them many times in our boat. These are wild and wonderfully romantic places, where pink flamingos settle in summer and Siberian wild ducks migrate to pass the winter, and where ruined palaces echo adventures from a time long past.

The Venetian lagoon, or what in Venice we call more simply *la laguna*, is that enclosed bay to the north of the Adriatic Sea, at the center of which the city itself floats. It's a stretch of deep green waters dotted with marshes, islands, and *bricole*—the wooden poles that act as markers for where you can and can't drive your boat, rather like roads in other cities. It is this body of water, however, that defines Venice, more even than the strict geographic limits of the city itself do. It is of the lagoon that Venice is born.

Above all, the lagoon dictates the way we eat in Venice: its waters have fed generations of Venetians and they feed us today. Mostly, the lagoon supplies fish and seafood, the real heart of Venetian cooking and the primary subject of this chapter. Of course, there is some meat: we have game and wild duck, pheasant, and *ucceletti* (small birds, like quail, larks, or even sparrows). These, too, come from the lagoon; in the winter months, many Venetians hunt for wild duck and the like, in boats specially decked out in camouflage to blend seamlessly with the scenery. And you will find, of course, a little beef and veal in Venetian cooking, usually in pasta sauce or slowly braised; otherwise, the diet is mostly fish. This makes the Venetian diet a largely healthy one, by happy accident rather than by any great design.

If and when you come to Venice, you will find many varieties of seafood particular to the lagoon, and you must be sure to taste them all. *Moeche* are the tiny soft-shell crabs that come into season only for a few weeks in late spring and early autumn. These are coated in a batter of eggs and flour and almost indecent amounts of Parmesan, before being deep-fried to make *moeche fritte*, what must be one of the most exquisite dishes in the Venetian culinary tradition. *Canoce* are quirky looking crustaceans that translate loosely in English to something like "mantis shrimp"; these must be eaten within hours of being caught and are thus nigh on impossible to export, though unspeakably sweet to eat—usually served raw, doused in olive oil and parsley. In a world where you can eat anything pretty much anywhere—Peruvian quinoa in New York and Chinese lychees in London—these are ingredients that through the sheer limitations of their geography I have come to think of as delicacies.

I have always loved to eat fish, but for a long time I felt apprehensive about cooking it: tentative about what to buy, uncertain about its freshness, oddly squeamish about the handling of it. But my husband adores fish, so I cooked fish because I love to cook for him. And then I began to cook fish because I loved to cook fish. I came round to the notion that fish is, in fact, the lazy cook's dream: remarkably low effort to prepare and very rewarding to eat. I discovered there is no great science to it: a fish that is fresh looks fresh. Its eyes are bright and sparkly, not cloudy; its body is firm; its scales are wet and glossy, not dry; its gills are red. It smells salty and briny like the seaside and not, as you might perhaps expect, "fishy." In fact, the less fresh the fish, the more pronounced its smell will be.

Whole salt-baked sea bass, clams sautéed with white wine and drenched in fresh parsley, langoustines either lightly poached and served with velvety homemade mayonnaise or fried with the finest and saltiest slivers of crispy potatoes—this is what I cook and love to eat. These are all dishes that celebrate *la laguna* in exquisitely simple, truly Venetian ways.

BAKED MUSSELS WITH BREAD CRUMBS AND LEMON

PEOCI AL PANGRATTATO E LIMONE

SERVES 4 TO 6, AS A SHARING PLATE

1 cup / 70g coarse dried bread crumbs

———

Small bunch of fresh flat-leaf parsley, leaves finely chopped

———

1 small garlic clove, finely chopped

———

Grated zest of ½ lemon

———

A generous pinch of salt

———

Freshly ground black pepper

———

2¼ pounds / 1kg fresh mussels

———

3 tablespoons olive oil

———

⅓ cup / 80g salted butter

———

MOST OFTEN, THIS DISH IS SERVED as an antipasto—just a couple of mussels on the shell enrobed in crisp bread crumbs and fresh herbs, small bite before the main dish gets under way. That said, I've been known to eat an entire plate of these as a meal, with anything from a green salad to roasted radicchio (see page 103) on the side.

When buying mussels, look for ones with tightly closed shells that smell fresh and briny like the seaside. Don't use those with cracked shells. Before cooking, tap any mussels with slightly open shells; if they don't close, then toss them out as well. You can store mussels in the fridge for a couple of days, though it is best to eat them as soon as possible after you buy them. If you do keep the mussels in the fridge, place them in a large bowl and cover with a damp tea towel to keep them moist and to let them breathe; don't store them in an airtight container, plastic bag, or water.

———

Preheat the oven to 350°F.

In a medium bowl, toss the bread crumbs, parsley, garlic, and lemon zest together. Season with salt and pepper to taste.

Rinse the mussels in a colander under cold running water, checking for cracked shells. If you buy the mussels from the supermarket, they most likely will already have been debearded, but if not, grab the beard (the short brown strings coming out of the mussel on one side) with your fingers and tug gently side to side, to detach it from the shell.

Heat 2 tablespoons of the olive oil in a pan large enough to fit the mussels set over medium heat. Add the mussels and cover the pan. Cook, giving the pan a good shake every now and then, until all the shells have opened, 3 minutes. Remove the pan from the heat and lift out the mussels, saving the cooking liquid. Remove and throw away one half shell from each mussel, and detach the mussel from the remaining shell to make them much easier to eat. Then spoon a little of the bread crumb mixture over each mussel in its shell, and arrange the shells on a baking sheet.

In a small saucepan set over low heat, melt the butter. Add the remaining tablespoon of olive oil, and then drizzle the mixture generously over all the mussels, trying to get as much buttery goodness into each shell as you can. Bake for 10 minutes, until the bread crumbs are golden.

As the mussels cook in the oven, bring the cooking liquid left in the pan to a simmer and cook to reduce it a little, about 5 minutes. Drizzle it over the mussels just before serving.

SCALLOPS ON THE SHELL WITH PISTACHIO GRATIN

CAPPE SANTE GRATINATE AL PISTACCHIO

SERVES 6 AS A STARTER

6 purchased scallop shells
(as for coquilles St. Jacques)

¼ cup (½ stick) / 50g salted butter

¼ cup / 25g shelled pistachios

⅓ cup / 20g coarse fresh
bread crumbs

A generous pinch of salt

6 firm sea scallops
(about ½ pound / 225g)

A loaf of crusty bread,
such as ciabatta or baguette

WE CELEBRATE CHRISTMAS both the Italian and the English way. On Christmas Eve, we feast on pasta dishes laden with truffles, whole fish baked in the oven, an array of local seafood, and panettone; on the day itself, we have roast turkey and plum pudding. For me, it would not be Christmas without a tray of scallops, cooked on the shell, topped with crisp bread crumbs and swimming in melted butter. That said, I certainly do not confine myself to eating these only at Christmas—I am far too greedy for that. This is a dish that lends itself just as well to dinner in the garden on a hot summer evening as to the bitter cold of the winter months.

I estimate one of these per person, when served as a starter, but I would always happily eat more. Make sure to serve them with bread for mopping up the buttery juices.

Preheat the oven to 400°F.

Arrange the scallop shells on a baking sheet; you will use these to serve the scallops.

Melt the butter in a small saucepan over gentle heat.

Toss the pistachios, bread crumbs, and a generous pinch of salt into a food processor and pulse until you have a coarse powder. Pour the mixture into a bowl and add the scallops. Roll the scallops in the bread crumb mixture so they are well coated, and then gently nestle each into the slightly depressed center of a scallop shell. Sprinkle generously with what is left of the bread crumb mixture. Spoon the melted butter over each of the scallops.

Bake for 12 to 15 minutes, until golden and bubbling on top. Serve with bread for mopping up the buttery juices.

CLAMS IN WHITE WINE SAUCE

VONGOLE SALTATE IN BIANCO

SERVES 4 AS A MAIN COURSE

4½ pounds / 2kg littleneck or cherrystone clams

¼ cup / 60 ml olive oil

2 garlic cloves, chopped

A pinch of salt

⅔ cup / 130ml dry white wine

A large bunch of fresh parsley, leaves chopped

A loaf of crusty bread, such as ciabatta or baguette

I CAN'T HELP BUT FEEL THAT clams are rather an unsung hero. While spaghetti alle vongole and variations upon that theme are commonplace on menus at restaurants across Venice, you don't see clams on the menu as often elsewhere. Yet I greatly prefer eating them to the more widely popular mussels: there is something more delicate and subtle about the flavor of clam meat.

This dish, which is rather like spaghetti alle vongole without the spaghetti, is synonymous for me with the food of my childhood. When you cook the clams this way, you don't waste a drop of their exquisite cooking juices, as you serve them still swimming in a heavenly broth of white wine, clam juices, grassy olive oil, garlic, and parsley. Mopping up the sauce with crusty white bread is the best part, so don't even think of eating this dish without any.

Like mussels, when you buy the clams, make sure they have tightly closed shells and cook them as soon as possible. Store in the fridge, in a large bowl, covered with a damp tea towel to keep them moist, but also to let them breathe.

Wash the clams thoroughly under cold running water. Check to see if any of the clams have open or broken shells, and discard them if they do.

Set a frying pan large enough to generously fit the clams over medium heat, and add the olive oil, garlic, and salt. Cook until the garlic has turned golden, 1 to 2 minutes; take care not to brown the garlic as it will turn bitter. Toss the clams into the pan and give them a good shake. Add the wine and let it bubble until all the clams have opened, about 4 or 5 minutes.

Sprinkle the parsley over the clams and serve immediately with crusty bread on the side.

POACHED LANGOUSTINES WITH SAFFRON MAYONNAISE

SCAMPI CON MAIONESE
ALLO ZAFFERANO

SERVES 4

½ teaspoon saffron threads

2 generous pinches of salt

2 large egg yolks

1 teaspoon Dijon mustard

A squeeze of lemon juice

½ cup / 100ml olive oil

½ cup / 100ml sunflower oil

20 langoustines
(roughly 4½ pounds / 2kg)

WHEN IT COMES TO LANGOUSTINES, those small edible lobsters, the effort lies mostly in the shopping. Not all fishmongers will sell them, and I have yet to see them at the supermarket; but if you give your fishmonger a heads-up a day or two beforehand, he should be able to obtain them for you–or you should easily be able to buy them frozen.

There are few things more delectable than sweet langoustines dipped into a creamy homemade mayonnaise (not, incidentally, to be confused with the store-bought mayo, which is a much lesser beast). If you have not made mayonnaise before, all you need is a good electric mixer or blender (or a handheld whisk and some serious elbow grease) and a modicum of patience. But if you don't have time to make the mayonnaise, then just cook the langoustines as below, roughly chop some parsley, and sprinkle it over the shells with a generous drizzle of good olive oil and a sprinkling of salt.

Begin by making the mayonnaise. Grind the saffron threads and a pinch of salt in a mortar and pestle until you have a fine powder.

In a medium bowl, combine the egg yolks, mustard, lemon juice, and a generous pinch of salt. Whisk vigorously, preferably with a handheld electric beater, until the yolks begin to turn a smooth, matte yellow, about 30 seconds. Now slowly pour in a few drops of the olive oil, beating all the while. As the oil blends into the egg, add a few more drops and keep going like that. As the mayonnaise begins to gain bulk, you can increase the speed at which you add the oil, so that eventually you are pouring a fine but constant stream of oil into the bowl as you whisk. If it looks like the mixture is about to split, stop adding the oil and keep whisking until it becomes smooth again; resume adding the rest of the olive oil, then add 1 tablespoon of cold water to stabilize it. Now, continue with the sunflower oil, pouring it into the bowl in a slow, steady stream. Taste the mayonnaise. Add a little more salt, if you like, then whisk in the saffron. (The mayonnaise will keep in the refrigerator for 2 days.)

Place a large pot of water on high heat and bring to a boil. Add a generous amount of salt; you want roughly 2 teaspoons per quart (L) of water. Working in batches, drop in the langoustines and cook for 1 minute. Use a slotted spoon to gently lift them out of the pan and set aside. To check if the langoustines are cooked, pull back their tails and look at the meat through the thin membrane; it should be white and opaque rather than translucent.

Either serve the langoustines straightaway while still warm or refrigerate until you are ready. I like to heap the langoustines on a plate, still in their shell, and let everyone help themselves, breaking into the shells and dipping the meat into the mayonnaise at the table.

SHRIMP BROTH

SERVES 4

1 small onion, finely chopped

1 medium carrot, finely chopped

1 celery stalk, finely chopped

1 small fennel bulb, finely chopped

1½ tablespoons olive oil

10 ounces / 300g jumbo shrimp,
peeled and deveined

A generous pinch of salt

Small bunch of fresh flat-leaf
parsley, leaves chopped

THIS IS A WONDERFULLY DELICATE DISH that is still somehow deeply comforting to eat. A lot of the flavor comes from the fresh vegetables that make up the broth's base—the fennel, in particular, gives a subtle but seductive hint of anise that I love. However, the real secret to making it well is to use really good shrimp: they should be fresh and plump and juicy, and bring a satisfying burst of flavor with each bite.

Pour 1 quart (1L) of water into a large saucepan set over high heat and bring to a boil. Add the onion, carrot, celery, and fennel; reduce the heat to medium and let simmer for 20 minutes.

Meanwhile, set a large frying pan over medium heat, and add the oil. Toss in the shrimp and a pinch of salt, and cook, turning them every now and then, until they have turned pink all over (but do not brown them), about 5 minutes.

Toss the shrimp into the pot of broth and cook for 5 more minutes. Sprinkle the parsley over the soup before serving.

LANGOUSTINE AND FIG SALAD

**SERVES 4 AS A STARTER OR
SHARING PLATE**

1 heaping teaspoon salt,
plus a generous pinch

12 langoustines
(roughly 2¼ pounds / 1kg)

¼ cup / 60 ml olive oil

Juice of ½ lemon

8 to 10 fresh figs, stemmed,
peeled, and quartered

A large bunch of fresh flat-leaf
parsley, leaves finely chopped

Freshly ground black pepper

IN OUR GARDEN GROWS A TALL, leafy fig tree. Under the dappled shade that it casts, we sit and eat our meals in the summertime, when the days are long and the air feels warm. Come the end of the summer, its fruit is ripe and for a few weeks of the year we find ourselves eating figs every which way: in tarts, over yogurt, poached in wine, in salads, with cream, and straight from the tree.

You need to trust me when it comes to pairing these two flavors. Think of it as a dish in the same vein as the more common prosciutto with melon, or prosciutto with fig, for that matter. If you like those, you will love this.

Fill a large saucepan with 1 quart (1L) of water, salt it generously, and bring to a boil over medium heat. Working in batches, drop in the langoustines. Cook for 1 minute, then use a slotted spoon to gently lift them out of the pan and set to one side. To check if the langoustines are cooked, pull back their tails and look at the meat through the thin membrane; it should be white and opaque rather than translucent. Let the langoustines cool, then peel and discard the shells. Arrange the langoustine meat on a large serving dish.

In a small bowl, make a vinaigrette by lightly whisking together the olive oil, lemon juice, and a generous pinch of salt. Arrange the figs on the langoustines, then drizzle it all with the vinaigrette. Sprinkle the parsley all over, season to taste with a little black pepper, and toss together before serving.

SHRIMP AND CHIPS

GAMBERONI CON PATATE

SERVES 4 AS A SHARING PLATE

4 medium russet potatoes
(roughly 1½ pounds / 680g)

Peanut oil, for frying

10 ounces / 300g jumbo shrimp,
peeled and deveined

Maldon or kosher salt

POTATO CHIPS—REALLY GOOD, SALTY HOMEMADE ONES—with fried jumbo shrimp may not sound like much, but I can't tell you what a firm favorite this recipe has become with every single member of our family.

They serve something very similar to this at Trattoria Quaranta Ladroni, an unassuming *trattoria* in the Cannaregio quarter in Venice. The dish comes as part of an array of seafood antipasti, which might be anything from char-grilled razor clams to polenta with *schie* (tiny brown shrimps), or deep-fried soft-shell crabs when they're in season. Pretty much whatever the chef fancies cooking is what you get. At home, I tend to do the same, if in a more moderate fashion: I might serve these alongside Scallops on the Shell with Pistachio Gratin (page 208), maybe with Poached Langoustines (page 212), or a Langoustine and Fig Salad (page 216). In the summer months, I may cook some Pan-Fried Artichoke Hearts with Parsley (page 75) and a nice plate of Slow-Cooked Peppers (page 98). I arrange everything on platters as sharing plates, casually plonked on the table for all of us to enjoy.

Using a mandoline or a very sharp knife, carefully slice the potatoes into rounds that are almost paper-thin. Fill a large bowl with cold water, drop the potato slices into it, and let them sit for at least 20 minutes so that they release some of their starch. (If you want to slice the potatoes ahead of time, you can keep them in cold water in the fridge overnight.)

Drain the potatoes in a colander and pat them dry with paper towels. Pour enough oil into a large, deep, heavy-bottomed pot (or use a deep-fryer) so that you have at least 2 to 3 inches of oil; make sure the oil does not fill the pan more than halfway. Heat the oil until it is 325° to 375°F. To test the heat, drop one potato slice into the oil; when bubbles form around it and it is really sizzling, you will know that your oil is hot enough for frying. If it blackens and burns, then the oil is too hot and you'll have to adjust the heat level accordingly.

Working in batches, and being careful not to crowd the pan, carefully add a few handfuls of the potato slices to the oil. Fry, turning them occasionally with a slotted spoon, until they are browned and crisp on both sides, about 4 minutes. Use a slotted spoon to lift them out and set them on paper towels to absorb excess oil. Repeat with the remaining potatoes.

Next, working in batches, add the shrimp to the oil. When they are pink on both sides, 1 to 2 minutes, use a slotted spoon to lift them out of the pan and set them on paper towels to absorb excess oil. Mix the shrimp with the potatoes, sprinkle generously with salt, and serve immediately.

OVEN-ROASTED STUFFED SARDINES

SARDE "QUASI IN SAOR"

SERVES 4 AS A MAIN COURSE

16 large whole sardines,
cleaned and filleted

2 tablespoons apple cider vinegar

4 to 5 dried bay leaves

1 teaspoon black peppercorns

2 tablespoons pine nuts

½ cup / 40g coarse fresh
bread crumbs

1 tablespoon plus 1 teaspoon
golden raisins

Juice of 1 lemon

3 tablespoons / 50ml olive oil

Scant ¼ cup / 50ml dry white wine

SARDINES ARE PLENTIFUL IN THE ADRIATIC, and we eat a lot of them in Venice. One of the most common ways, and one of the most famous traditional Venetian preparations, is what we call *in saor*. This term refers to a method of lightly dusting sardines in flour, then pan-frying them and serving in a sauce of vinegar, bay leaves, peppercorns, raisins, and pine nuts (much like the recipe for roasted pumpkin on page 97). Here is a fresh, slightly mellower play on those same flavors, in which I've stuffed the sardines with raisins, pine nuts, and plenty of bread crumbs, splashed them with white wine, and roasted them gently in the oven. These are light and fresh, and I might serve them with anything from a crisp green salad—dressed with a drizzle of olive oil, squeeze of lemon, and pinch of salt—in the summer, to a generous dollop of runny polenta (see page 000) in the winter.

Preheat the oven to 425°F.

Lay the fillets in a large baking dish, drizzle the vinegar over them, crumble in the bay leaves and sprinkle the peppercorns on top. Cover and let rest for about 30 minutes.

Roughly chop 1½ tablespoons of the pine nuts (saving the rest for later) and put them in a large bowl with the bread crumbs and approximately 1 tablespoon of the raisins. Squeeze in most of the lemon juice, then drizzle in 1 to 2 tablespoons of the olive oil. You want to make a stiff stuffing; if it feels too soft, add more bread crumbs.

Remove the bay leaves and peppercorns from the fish, carefully spoon a layer of the stuffing over the top of half the fillets, then sandwich on top of each stuffed fillet a second fillet of fish. Drizzle the remaining tablespoon of olive oil and the remaining lemon juice over the fish, and pour over the white wine. Sprinkle on the remaining ½ tablespoon of pine nuts and 1 teaspoon of raisins, and cover the dish with foil.

Roast for 5 minutes. Remove the foil and bake for 5 minutes more, until cooked through. Gently lift each stuffed sardine out of the roasting dish and arrange on a platter before serving.

OVEN-ROASTED PORGY WITH ALMONDS AND FIGS

ORATA AL FORNO CON FICHI E MANDORLE

SERVES 4 AS A MAIN COURSE

4 whole porgies, cleaned (about 12 ounces /340g each)

Salt

10 dried figs, quartered

½ cup / 80g pitted black olives

2 tablespoons / 20g chopped almonds

¼ cup / 50ml dry white wine

¼ cup / 50ml olive oil

A few sprigs of fresh rosemary

THERE ARE SO MANY COMPLEX and delightful flavors in this dish—the salty olives, the sweet figs, and the heady aroma of rosemary that runs throughout—that it makes for a sumptuous meal all by itself. I would serve it with nothing more than a light salad.

Depending on the size of the fish you purchase, one per person should work. Also, I always insist on bringing the fish to the table whole, still in their roasting pan, so everyone can enjoy them with their eyes, before I fillet and serve. Ask your fishmonger to clean the fish so they are ready to cook.

Preheat the oven to 350°F.

Rinse the fish under cold running water, then pat dry with paper towels and lay them out in a roasting pan. Take care to pat dry their insides, then rub the insides with a little salt. Toss the figs, olives, and almonds into the pan, scattering them over and among the fish. Drizzle in the wine and olive oil, then tear the rosemary into pieces and toss them into the roasting pan.

Roast for 25 to 30 minutes, until the fish are cooked; the flesh should be opaque and feel tender when touched with a knife. Serve the fish hot, either filleted for your guests or whole, as they prefer.

SOLE IN SAFFRON SAUCE

SOGLIOLE SAPORITE ALLO ZAFFERANO

SERVES 4 AS A MAIN COURSE

6 tablespoons (¾ stick) / 75g salted butter

4 sole fillets (about 4½ ounces / 125g each)

A generous pinch of salt

Freshly ground black pepper

Small bunch of fresh parsley, leaves chopped

Small bunch of fresh thyme, leaves chopped

3 to 4 dried bay leaves

½ cup / 120ml dry white wine

½ teaspoon saffron threads

2 teaspoons all-purpose flour

2 tablespoons light cream

ONE OF THE THINGS THAT SETS Venetian cooking apart from most other Italian food is the way it uses spices. The Venetian Republic was a state of merchants; it was built largely on trade, and it welcomed ingredients and influences, culinary and otherwise, from the cultures it traded with. It is the saffron here that elevates an otherwise lean and simple dish of baked sole fillets.

I find the saffron-hued, buttery, white wine sauce to be quite rich, so the quantities are a little on the scant side, so as not to overwhelm the fish. That said, feel free to whip up more sauce if you like.

This is particularly nice served with plain steamed green asparagus, a Garden Pea and Almond Salad (page 94), or Spinach with Pine Nuts and Raisins (page 79).

Preheat the oven to 350°F.

In a small saucepan set over medium heat, melt 5 tablespoons (60g) of the butter.

Arrange the sole fillets skin side down in a large baking dish. Sprinkle with a little salt, pepper, parsley, thyme, and the bay leaves. Drizzle the melted butter and the wine over the fish, then cover the dish with foil.

Bake for 10 to 12 minutes, until the fillets are cooked through; the flesh should be flaky and opaque. Gently lift the fillets onto a serving dish, and cover with foil to keep them warm while you make the sauce.

Pour the cooking juices from the baking dish into a small saucepan. Set the pan over medium heat, add the remaining tablespoon (15g) of butter and the saffron threads, and warm gently. When the butter is melted, add the flour, stirring constantly with a wooden spoon until smooth, then add the cream. Cook for about 2 minutes to allow the flavors to meld, then pour the sauce over the fish and serve immediately.

SALT-BAKED SEA BASS

BRANZINO AL SALE

SERVES 4 AS A MAIN COURSE

5 pounds / 2kg rock salt

1 medium sea bass
(about 1½ pounds / 750g), cleaned
and with head and tail on

Small bunch of fresh flat-leaf
parsley

Small bunch of fresh thyme

1 lemon, sliced

Olive oil, for serving

I LOVE THE SENSE OF THEATER that cooking fish in a salt crust creates. I insist on bringing the fish to the table whole and still in its salt casing so I can dramatically crack it open for everyone.

If you can, try to obtain a wild-caught sea bass. They tend to be larger, more expensive, and trickier to get hold of than their farmed counterparts, which are widely available—but the wild ones are also considerably more flavorsome. If you prefer, you can also cook porgy this way; just adjust the cooking time to match the weight of the fish, bearing in mind that you should allow roughly 10 minutes per 1 inch of thickness. As for estimating quantity, I tend to err on the side of generosity, as I have a soft spot for leftover sea bass, served cold with a drizzle of olive oil the next day. Serve this with either a rich and creamy Gratin of Fennel (page 91) or something light, such as Roasted Celery with Cherry Tomatoes and Pancetta (page 80)—or better still, serve it with both.

Preheat the oven to 400°F. Line a roasting pan with parchment paper.

In a large bowl, combine the rock salt with 1 cup (200ml) water, using your hands to create a thick paste. Spread some of the salt paste over the paper lining in an even layer ½ to ¾ inch (1 to 2cm) thick.

Rinse the fish by running it under cold water, then pat it dry with a paper towel. Lay the fish on top of the salt, and fill its cavity with the parsley, thyme, and lemon slices. Cover the fish with the rest of the salt paste, molding it around the fish with your hands and pressing down gently so the crust adheres. Leave the head and the tail uncovered.

Bake for 20 minutes. To serve, cut away the salt crust, then skin and fillet the fish for serving. Eat warm or at room temperature with a drizzle of olive oil.

OVEN-ROASTED TURBOT WITH POTATOES, OLIVES, AND CHERRY TOMATOES

ROMBO AL FORNO CON PATATE, OLIVE, E POMODORINI

SERVES 4 AS A MAIN COURSE

3 to 4 medium potatoes (roughly
1½ pounds / 680g), sliced about
¼ inch (5 mm) thick

3 tablespoons / 50ml olive oil

1 garlic clove, crushed

Small bunch of fresh thyme,
leaves pulled off

Salt and freshly ground black pepper

2¼ pounds / 1kg whole turbot,
cleaned and with head and
tail left on

10 to 12 black olives, pitted
and chopped

10 to 12 cherry tomatoes,
chopped

½ cup / 100 ml dry white wine

OF COURSE, IT'S HARD TO GO WRONG with crisp oven-roasted potatoes. But this particular recipe—for which you cook the potatoes beneath the fish so they soak up all the flavor—really exceeds all expectations.

You should be able to buy fresh turbot from your local fishmonger, especially if requested in advance. However, if you can't find turbot, then large whole sole or fluke (summer flounder) is more widely available and makes for a good alternative.

Preheat the oven to 400°F.

Arrange the potato slices in the bottom of a baking pan large enough to fit the whole fish. You want a single layer of overlapping potato slices. Drizzle the potatoes with the olive oil and toss in the garlic. Sprinkle generously with the thyme leaves, salt, and pepper.

Roast for 15 to 20 minutes, until lightly browned and crisp. Remove the pan from the oven and turn the heat down to 350°F.

Lay the turbot over the potatoes. Season the fish with a little salt and pepper. Scatter the olives and tomatoes around the fish. Roast for 20 minutes. Remove the baking pan from the oven, pour the wine over the fish and potatoes, and continue to roast for 15 to 20 more minutes, until the fish falls away easily from the bone when you insert a small knife. Serve hot.

MEAT, SAGE, AND APPLE SKEWERS

OSEI SCAMPAI

MAKES 6 TO 8 SKEWERS, FOR 4 SERVINGS

2 skinless chicken breast halves, (about 8 ounces / 225g), cut into bite-size pieces

———

12 ounces / 320g boneless pork loin, trimmed of all fat and cut into bite-size pieces

———

4 ounces /120g pancetta, sliced into bite-size pieces

———

2 medium apples, cored, quartered, and cut into thick half-moon slices

———

Large bunch of fresh sage, leaves torn

———

3 tablespoons / 50ml olive oil

———

½ cup / 100ml dry white wine

———

Dijon or whole-grain mustard, for serving

———

WE CALL THIS *OSEI SCAMPAI* in Venice, which is a phrase in dialect that translates loosely as "the little birds that got away." It's a nod to the custom of hunting small birds—blackbirds, larks, sparrows, pretty much anything small that sings—to cook and eat. This custom of hunting tiny birds is now outdated, so these skewers—made with a mix of grilled meats—represent "the ones that got away." I have used chicken, pork loin, and pancetta, but veal, beef, or Italian sausage all work very well, too, and are common alternatives. To the meat, I've added slices of apple; the fruit caramelizes deliciously in the wine and meat juices, and pays a very sweet complement to the pork. Whatever you do, make sure to serve this with copious quantities of mustard.

Thread the chicken, pork, pancetta, and apple on wooden skewers, alternating each piece of chicken or meat with a sage leaf. There is no right or wrong way to do this, but I like to include 3 pieces of apple on each skewer, and then a roughly equal balance of pork and chicken, with a couple of pieces of pancetta thrown in for good measure.

Set a large skillet over medium heat and add the oil. Working in batches, arrange the skewers in the pan, taking care not to overcrowd the pan, and cook, turning the skewers every now and then so they color evenly, until browned on all sides, 6 to 8 minutes. Pour in the wine, let it bubble for 2 minutes, then lower the heat to medium-low and cover the pan. Let simmer until the sauce is largely reduced and the meat is cooked through, 8 to 10 minutes.

Serve with strong mustard.

ROAST DUCK WITH APPLES, PEARS, AND CHESTNUTS

ANATRA AL FORNO
CON MELE, PERE,
E CASTAGNE

SERVES 4

1 duckling (4¼ pounds / 2kg)

2 medium apples, cored
and chopped

2 shallots, chopped

Small bunch of sage, leaves torn

Juice of ½ lemon

Salt

Freshly ground black pepper

¼ cup / 70ml brandy

4 pears, peeled, cored,
and quartered

1 cup / 150g boiled chestnuts

THE IDEA TO TOSS A FEW brandy-drenched slices of pear and a handful of chestnuts in the pan along with the duck is not mine—it must be credited to the classic Venetian cookbook *A Tòla co i Nostri Veci*. The deliciously caramelized fruit is a marvelous match for the meat.

My instructions for preparing the duck here are, I concede, a little laborious. But the extra steps are entirely necessary, as they allow the skin to crisp up beautifully when roasted in the oven.

Bring a large pot of water to a boil.

Pierce the skin of the duck all over with a fork. Set the duck on a wire roasting rack in the sink, then pour the boiling water over it. Pat dry with paper towels. Set the bird still on the wire rack in a roasting pan and refrigerate it for 2 hours to dry out the skin.

Toss the apples, shallots, and sage in a large bowl, then squeeze the lemon juice over it all. Season with a little salt and pepper, and pour in half the brandy. Stir and let steep for at least 10 to 15 minutes.

Some 20 minutes before you are ready to roast the duck, preheat the oven to 400°F and take the bird out of the fridge to bring it to room temperature (if it is too cold, it will affect its cooking time).

Fill the duck's cavity with the apple stuffing, then generously rub the skin of the bird all over with salt.

Roast for 30 minutes. Remove the pan from the oven and carefully drain the duck fat into a heat-resistant bowl. Return the pan to the oven and reserve the duck fat for another time (it's particularly delicious for roasting potatoes). Roast the duck for 30 more minutes. Remove the pan from the oven and arrange the pear chunks around the duck. Pour the remaining brandy over the pears and put the pan back in the oven to roast for another 30 minutes. Toss the chestnuts in the bottom of the roasting pan and roast for 35 to 45 more minutes, until the bird's juices run clear.

Let the duck rest for 15 to 20 minutes before serving. Serve with the brandied pears and chestnuts, as well as the heavenly apple and sage stuffing.

ROASTED DUCK LEGS WITH PLUMS

COSCE D'ANATRA AL FORNO CON PRUGNE

SERVES 4

1 tablespoon olive oil

4 duck legs (roughly 8 ounces / 220g each)

Salt

Freshly ground black pepper

8 plums, halved and pitted

Small bunch of fresh thyme

IN THE WINTER MONTHS, wild ducks migrate from Russia to the Venetian lagoon. There is, in fact, a wonderfully evocative passage in Hemingway's novel *Across the River and Into the Trees*, in which he describes the logistics of shooting duck from wooden boats in the lagoon. Some sixty years on and counting, little has changed. Of course, this recipe can be made with domestic duck, which is a bit juicier and milder tasting.

Duck is one of my favorite meats both to cook (very forgiving) and to eat (very flavorsome). This recipe requires a longer cooking time than many others, but impinges very little upon you as cook. I like to brown the legs, skin side down, a little first before I roast them, as I find brown, crisp duck skin to be one of life's great pleasures. The recipe calls for plums; the sharpness of the fruit pairs seductively with the rich, gamey meat. That said, roasted grapes, and even peaches, would be every bit as exquisite.

Preheat the oven to 400°F.

Drizzle the oil into a large casserole dish or heatproof baking pan and set it over medium heat. Season the duck legs with a little salt and pepper, then arrange them in the pan and cook, skin side down, until the skin becomes crisp and golden, 7 to 8 minutes. Remove the pan from the heat and turn the duck legs over.

Roast the duck legs for 1 hour. Remove the pan from the oven, and arrange the plum halves snugly around the browned legs. Sprinkle with a few sprigs of thyme, and a pinch of salt and pepper, and set back into the oven.

Roast for 40 more minutes. The skin should be crisp, but the meat deliciously tender, and the fruit sticky and almost caramelized on top.

SAGE AND BUTTER ROASTED PHEASANT

FAGIANO AL FORNO CON
BURRO E SALVIA

SERVES 2

3 tablespoons / 50ml olive oil

¼ cup (½ stick) / 50g salted butter

Small bunch of sage

1 pheasant (about 1⅓ pounds / 600g), dressed

Salt

Freshly ground black pepper

¾ cup / 150ml vegetable broth

¼ cup / 60ml dry white wine

YOU CAN HUNT PHEASANT, along with wild duck and other game, in the marshes of the Venetian lagoon. And because it is locally and readily available, it makes regular appearances on the Venetian dining table. This method of roasting the bird, drenched in melted butter and white wine, ensures that the meat (which can otherwise be a little tough) is tender to eat. Serve with a nice salad (something like a red chicory with mustard dressing would work well), Roasted Radicchio with Pomegranate (page 103), or Roasted Pumpkin with Onions, Raisins, and Pine Nuts (page 97) for an ideal for supper for two. Though, of course, you could just as easily roast two, three, or four birds were you cooking for four, six, or eight, respectively.

Preheat the oven to 350°F.

In a large, heavy-bottomed casserole or Dutch oven, add the olive oil, half the butter, and three-fourths of the sage leaves. Set the pan on medium heat until the butter is melted, 1 to 2 minutes. Season the pheasant with a little salt and pepper, then add the bird to the pan and cook, turning it every now and then, until browned on all sides, 10 to 15 minutes. Take more time to brown the legs, as these cook slower than the breast.

Meanwhile, in a small saucepan set over medium heat, bring the vegetable broth to a boil.

Remove the pheasant from the pan, wipe the browned butter and oil out with some paper towels, and discard the very dark sage. Then place the pan back over medium heat, add the remaining butter and sage, put the pheasant back in, and then pour in the wine. Let it bubble for 2 minutes before adding the hot broth.

Place the pheasant in the oven and roast for 20 minutes, until the juices from the leg run clear. Let the bird rest for 10 minutes before serving, then carve and drizzle the cooking juices over the meat.

LA PASTICCERIA

DESSERTS
AND SWEET TREATS

WHILE TO BUY YOUR PASTA SAUCE in a jar might be frowned upon by Italian *nonne*, to buy fine pastries from a good bakery is fair game. The making of these sorts of ornate sweets is, broadly speaking, felt to be a business best left to those who really know how to do it. *Pasticcerie* are, with very few exceptions, family-run businesses, and the trade of fine baking is passed down through generations. It is an art. To visit *la pasticceria*—with its trays upon trays of delicate confections brimming with cream and dusted with confectioners' sugar, all impressively lined up behind the glass counter—is in itself worth traveling to Italy for.

The Venetian way of doing sweets is every bit as distinctive as their way of doing fish, pasta, polenta, or *cicheti*. It is highly regional, and laced with the influences of the city's rich history. Look closely, and in the array of sweets on display at *pasticcerie* throughout town, you will find a narrative every bit as rich as that painted in the Byzantine mosaics of San Marco or Napoleon's Venetian palaces. Dark chocolate Sacher tortes topped with wonderfully fine decoration, and slices of spiced apple strudel, for example, are firm staples at *pasticcerie*: they are a legacy left behind by the Austrians in the nineteenth century that has come now to be a cornerstone of Venetian culinary heritage. Alongside these most likely you will find choux pastry puffs laced with Venetian zabaione custard (and often in the shape of miniature swans); and when it is Carnival season, you will see *Frittelle* (page 247) and *Galani* (page 258) piled high on trays atop the counters at *pasticcerie*. These are Venetian treats that date back to the city's heyday as the Serenissima Republic and are still popular today.

At Christmastime, the good *pasticcerie* will bake their own panettone. Each shop has its own way of doing it. Plain and peppered with candied peel and raisins versions are widely available, but at Pasticceria Rosa Salva, a Venetian institution, they lace the panettone with marzipan, enrobe it with fondant icing, and then top it with sugar-dipped roses and violets. At Pasticceria Didovich, a particular favorite of mine, they layer the soft panettone with wild berry jam, then drape it in dark chocolate and decorate with gold leaf. Pastry of this kind is a fine art. Like much of life in Venice, it feels like something from a bygone era: slightly dated, but all the more precious for it. These shop windows, breathtaking as they are, are as much about showing off as they are about enchanting and pleasing. They are showmanship.

I bake at home a lot. But the kind of baking I do is at polar opposites from the ornate virtuosity you find in a *pasticceria*. Home baking for me fills a different need and purpose. It is not about impressing, any more than it is a business confined to formal occasions; it is about comforting and delighting.

I firmly believe that when it comes to sweets, homemade is second to none. To eat a cake that has been baked for you—and just for you—somehow makes you feel cosseted and nurtured. Better still, to bake a cake for someone else is deeply gratifying, however simple the recipe might be or however higgledy-piggledy the cake might turn out. Of all the world's culinary truths, I find this one to be universal: food is nostalgia as much as it is nourishment. And never, somehow, does this prove so true as when it comes to the matter of baked goods.

Much of what I bake is inspired by what you will find in a *pasticceria*, but in my home kitchen it takes a simpler, less refined form: ricotta cake, creamy and peppered with brandy-drenched raisins, but without even a hint of decoration; snow-white meringues, crisp on the outside and deliciously gooey at their center, not in the form of delicate swans but roughly shaped as they fall from my spoon onto the baking sheet; *crostate*, or jam tarts, with imperfectly crimped pastry edges; and chocolate cake, birthday cake, Christmas cake. I still can't tear myself away from the notion that a birthday cake is not a proper birthday cake unless it is made at home. Nor, for that matter, would I ever want to.

PEACHES POACHED IN AMARETTO SYRUP

PESCE ALL'AMARETTO

SERVES 6

1¼ cups / 300ml amaretto liqueur

½ cup / 100g granulated sugar

6 firm peaches, halved and pitted

THIS IS A DESSERT THAT WILL FOREVER be associated in my mind with lunches in our garden, in the deep heat of late summer. I feel quite strongly that it should be served chilled, with the fruit swimming in its syrup of sugar and amaretto liqueur, and a dollop of mascarpone cheese or vanilla ice cream perhaps, spooned generously on top. Be mindful when choosing your peaches to err on the side of slightly underripe fruit: you want whole peaches that are still firm, almost hard, so they will hold their shape well as they cook gently. The flesh of the cooked peaches turns a magical amber color, reminiscent of a tropical sunset—or in the case of white peaches, a seductive blushing pink.

In a large saucepan set over medium heat, combine 3 cups (650ml) cold water, the amaretto, and the sugar; heat, stirring occasionally, until the sugar dissolves, 2 to 3 minutes. Bring the syrup to a gentle boil, and lower the fruit into the pan so that they fit snugly. Most likely you will need to do this in two batches. Gently cook the fruit for about 5 minutes on one side, then use a spoon to turn it over and cook for about 5 more minutes on the other side. How long the peaches will take to cook depends very much on how ripe the fruit is and on how you like to eat it: I prefer my peaches firm, barely cooked at all, just infused with the sweet syrup, whereas my husband likes them so tender they melt in his mouth. You can test how cooked the fruit is by inserting a fork into their cut undersides (I do this at the hollow from the stone, so you barely notice the fork marks).

When the peaches are cooked, remove the pan from the heat and let them cool in the syrup. If you are cooking the peaches in batches, gently lift the cooked fruit out of the pan and set to one side while you poach the rest of the fruit in what is left of the syrup. When the peaches become cool enough to touch, remove them from the syrup and gently peel off their skins. Arrange them, cut side down, in a bowl and cover with the boozy syrup. Refrigerate for at least 20 to 30 minutes before serving. (The peaches will keep, swimming in their syrup and in a bowl covered with plastic wrap, for 2 days.)

RAISIN AND PINE NUT SUGAR DOUGHNUTS WITH WHIPPED RICOTTA CREAM

FRITTELLE ALLA VENEZIANA
CON CREMA ALLA RICOTTA

MAKES 14 TO 16 SMALL FRITTELLE

FOR THE FRITTELLE

¾ cup / 100g raisins

⅓ cup / 50g candied peel of choice, chopped

1½ tablespoons / 25ml grappa or other eau-de-vie

3½ tablespoons / 50g salted butter, cut into pieces

⅔ cup / 150ml whole milk

2 cups / 250g bread flour

7 tablespoons / 85g granulated sugar

1½ teaspoons instant yeast

¼ teaspoon salt

1 large egg

⅓ cup / 50g pine nuts

Peanut oil, for frying

FOR THE RICOTTA CREAM

1 cup plus 2 tablespoons / 250g ricotta

⅓ cup / 40g confectioners' sugar

STRICTLY SPEAKING, CARNIVAL IN VENICE begins the day after Epiphany (January 6th) and runs right through to the start of Lent. It really heats up, though, in the fortnight before Shrove Tuesday–that is when you see many people wandering the streets in full costume, wearing ornate capes and even more extravagant masks. It is a time for celebration and for excess, and the entire city–from children to *nonni* and everyone in between–get into the spirit of it.

With the beginning of Carnival come *frittelle*–sweet doughnuts that are light as air and peppered with pine nuts, raisins, and candied peel. Handwritten signs go up in the windows of the *pasticcerie* that read "*frittelle oggi*," meaning "frittelle made fresh today"; they are little needed, as you can smell their glorious doughy scent from far away. Frittelle come either plain (the so-called *alla Veneziana*), or filled with zabaione, chocolate custard, or (my favorite) ricotta cream. I don't bother filling them at home; it's too messy and I find they tend to go soggy if not eaten straightaway. Instead, I plonk the frittelle down on the table along with a big bowl of whipped ricotta for us all to spoon and dip as we like.

Make the frittelle. Toss the raisins and candied peel into a small bowl, pour over the grappa, cover the bowl with a clean tea towel, and set aside to steep.

In a small saucepan set over low heat, combine the butter and milk. Warm the mixture until the butter starts to melt, 1 to 2 minutes. Remove the pan from the heat, and stir with a wooden spoon. You want the butter melted and the milk warmed, but you don't want it to be too hot when you add the yeast. You should be able to dip your finger in the milk and hold it there, and for it to feel warm but by no means hot.

In a large bowl, combine the flour, 2 tablespoons (25g) of the sugar, the yeast, and the salt. Make a well in the center of the mixture. Crack the egg into the well, then pour in the warm milk mixture. Use your hands to bring the ingredients together into a dough. Turn it out onto a floured surface and knead until the dough feels smooth and elastic in your hands, about 10 minutes. If you tear off a small piece, roughly the size of a golf ball, you should be able to stretch it between your fingers into a sheet that is thin enough for you to see the light through. If the dough tears as you stretch it, then it needs a little more kneading. Roll the dough into a large ball, set it back in the bowl, cover with a clean tea towel, and put the bowl in a warm place for the dough to rise until doubled in size, about 45 minutes.

recipe continues

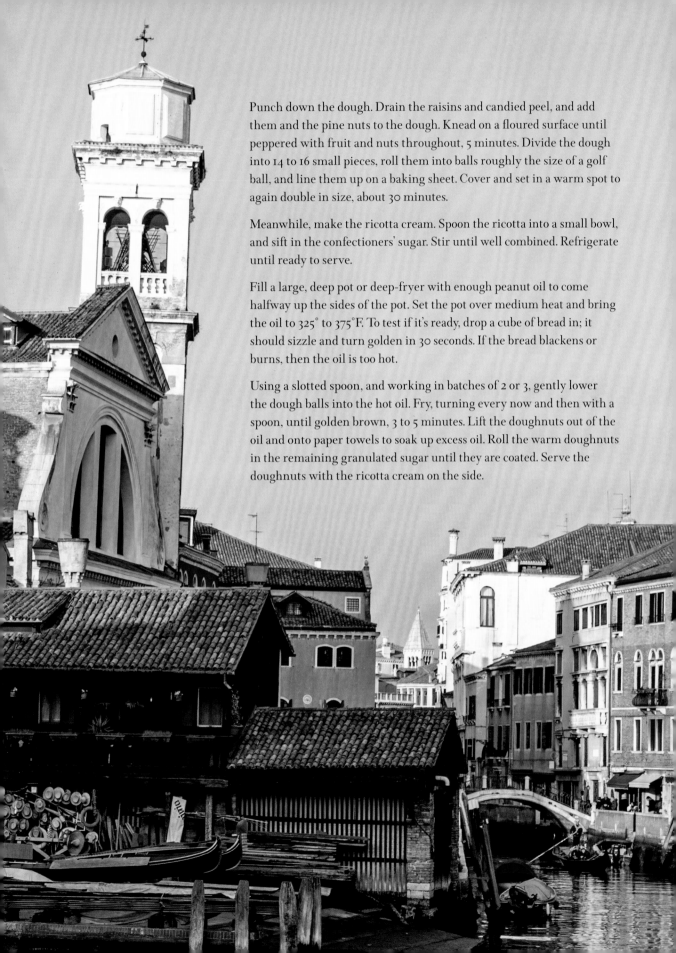

Punch down the dough. Drain the raisins and candied peel, and add them and the pine nuts to the dough. Knead on a floured surface until peppered with fruit and nuts throughout, 5 minutes. Divide the dough into 14 to 16 small pieces, roll them into balls roughly the size of a golf ball, and line them up on a baking sheet. Cover and set in a warm spot to again double in size, about 30 minutes.

Meanwhile, make the ricotta cream. Spoon the ricotta into a small bowl, and sift in the confectioners' sugar. Stir until well combined. Refrigerate until ready to serve.

Fill a large, deep pot or deep-fryer with enough peanut oil to come halfway up the sides of the pot. Set the pot over medium heat and bring the oil to 325° to 375°F. To test if it's ready, drop a cube of bread in; it should sizzle and turn golden in 30 seconds. If the bread blackens or burns, then the oil is too hot.

Using a slotted spoon, and working in batches of 2 or 3, gently lower the dough balls into the hot oil. Fry, turning every now and then with a spoon, until golden brown, 3 to 5 minutes. Lift the doughnuts out of the oil and onto paper towels to soak up excess oil. Roll the warm doughnuts in the remaining granulated sugar until they are coated. Serve the doughnuts with the ricotta cream on the side.

STRAWBERRY AND VODKA SORBET

SGROPPINO ALLA FRAGOLA

SERVES 6

½ lemon

1 large egg white

2½ cups / 400g strawberry sorbet

Scant ¼ cup / 50ml chilled vodka

¾ cup / 200ml chilled Prosecco or other sparkling white wine

SGROPPINO IS HALFWAY BETWEEN a digestivo and a pudding, made by blending a sharp sorbet with a dash of vodka and a glass of Prosecco. Most commonly you would mix it with lemon sorbet, though I have had it with all manner of flavors—grapefruit, licorice, and coffee, to name just a few. Strawberry is my particular favorite, if only because of its blushing pink color. It's a lovely, light way to end a meal—just a touch of sweet to finish everything off, perhaps with a few cookies for dipping (the Zaletti, page 61, would be ideal). I find that no matter how indulgent or filling the main course has been, there is always room for a sgroppino.

Rub the lemon over the inside of a bowl to remove any traces of grease. Then whisk the egg white with a handheld electric mixer until stiff, 3 to 5 minutes. Put the egg white in a blender and add the sorbet, vodka, and Prosecco. Blend until smooth and fluffy.

Pour into a pitcher or individual glasses, and refrigerate for up to 4 hours. Serve chilled, as you would a cocktail.

SAFFRON PANNA COTTA

PANNACOTTA ALLO ZAFFERANO

SERVES 4

1 (¼ ounce) package / 2 sheets of unflavored gelatin

¾ teaspoon saffron threads

A pinch of salt

2 cups / 500ml heavy cream

½ cup / 80g granulated sugar

TO ME, PANNA COTTA IS COMFORT FOOD. It is best eaten with no rigmarole, spooned greedily straight out of the cup or glass in which it was chilling in the fridge. And now that I have spared you the anxiety of turning panna cotta out of a mold and hoping it will hold its shape (which I always find inordinately stressful), you will find that there are few dishes easier to make. This recipe is almost farcical in its simplicity; thick cream, sugar, and a little gelatin to help the pudding set. Or, ideally, barely set: I like mine best when it has the texture of soft thickened cream.

I have added a touch of saffron here, which gives a delicate, almost floral undertone to the cream and, of course, also turns it an irresistible shade of deep yellow. In summertime, I serve this with a bowl of fresh red berries and nothing more. You can use saffron threads as they are, but I find that if you use a pestle and mortar to grind them into a fine powder, the cream develops a richer yellow hue with flecks of deep orange through it.

Put the gelatin in a small bowl, cover with ¼ cup (60ml) cold water, and allow it to soften, 5 minutes.

Use a pestle and mortar to grind the saffron threads and salt until you have a fine powder.

In a heavy-bottomed saucepan set over low heat, combine the cream and sugar. Heat, stirring regularly with a wooden spoon, until the cream is just about to boil (you will see a little steam coming off the pan and the tiniest of bubbles floating to the top of the cream at the edges of the pan), 10 to 12 minutes. Remove the pan from the heat.

Add the gelatin to the saucepan and stir vigorously until dissolved. Then add the saffron powder and stir until well combined. Pour the mixture into serving glasses, custard cups, or a large bowl—whatever takes your fancy and you have on hand. Refrigerate the panna cotta for 4 hours, until set. Serve cold.

CHOCOLATE AND AMARETTO CUSTARD

CREMA AL CIOCCOLATO CON AMARETTI

SERVES 4

3 tablespoons / 25g
all-purpose flour

¾ cup / 60g unsweetened
cocoa powder

½ cup / 90g granulated sugar

A generous pinch of salt

2 cups / 500ml whole milk

15 / 80g crisp amaretti cookies

THIS IS THAT ELUSIVE TREAT: a recipe you can whip up at the last minute, without making a trip to the store for supplies. That it is made from cupboard ingredients and is so simple to prepare shouldn't, however, take away from how good it tastes: it is chocolatey, much as you would expect, but also beautifully light and airy.

I've layered the custard with a few roughly broken amaretti cookies, and the crisp hint of sweet almond is particularly good with the smooth, dark chocolate. You could also serve the custard plain, unadulterated in its chocolatey-ness, or with a crumbling of anything from shortbread to gingersnaps on top.

In a heavy-bottomed saucepan set over medium heat, combine the flour, cocoa, sugar, and salt. Pour in the milk and stir with a wooden spoon. Set the pan over medium-low heat and cook, stirring continuously until the custard begins to thicken, about 5 minutes. Remove the pan from the heat and let cool for about 5 minutes; it will thicken a little as it cools.

Crumble half the amaretti cookies into 4 small cups, bowls, or ramekins (I like to use teacups), distributing the crumbles equally among the cups. Spoon the thick chocolate cream over the crumbles. Let cool, then refrigerate until cold, 20 to 30 minutes. Before serving, crumble the remaining amaretti over the top of each serving.

MARIA'S FAMOUS TIRAMISÙ

IL FAMOSO TIRAMISÙ
DI MARIA

SERVES 8

½ lemon

4 large eggs

¾ cup / 120g granulated sugar

2½ cups / 600g mascarpone

26 to 28 / 225g ladyfingers

2 cups / 450ml strong
coffee, cooled

Unsweetened cocoa powder,
for dusting

AS MUCH AS I WOULD LIKE to take credit for it, this is my friend Maria's recipe for tiramisù—unadulterated and unchanged. Of all the recipes in this book, this one probably means the most to me. Tiramisù was the first thing I ever cooked for my husband, and I like to believe that there, over spoonfuls of whipped mascarpone cream and sugar cookies dipped in coffee, began a great love story.

As with most trifles, depending on the shape and size of the bowl you are planning to serve it from, you will want to think in terms of layers: a layer of ladyfingers drenched in strong coffee and smothered in the airy mascarpone custard, then a second layer of cookies, more coffee and more custard, all dusted in cocoa powder. Take this recipe as a guide and scale it as you like; you really can't go wrong. If I find myself with any leftover mascarpone custard, I keep it in a pitcher in the fridge and eat it with fresh fruit the next day. And bear in mind that tiramisù improves a little with time, so if you can, make it a day ahead of when you're planning to serve it.

Rub the lemon over the inside of a medium mixing bowl to remove any traces of grease. Separate the eggs and add the egg whites to the prepared bowl. Add the yolks to another bowl, add half of the sugar, and whisk until light and fluffy, 2 to 3 minutes. Use a wooden spoon to stir in the mascarpone.

Use an electric mixer to beat the egg whites on medium-low speed until they begin to froth, 1 to 2 minutes. Increase the speed to high and begin adding the remaining sugar a spoonful at a time until the whites become glossy and begin to form stiff peaks, 3 to 4 minutes. Fold the whites into the yolks.

Line the bottom of a 2-quart (1.7L) glass serving bowl or dish with half the ladyfingers; if needed, break some into smaller pieces and wedge them in to fill any small gaps. Pour half the coffee over the cookies and use your fingers to press the cookies down so they soak up the liquid. Spoon half the custard over the coffee-soaked biscuits and spread it evenly with a knife or spatula. Then add another layer of ladyfingers, pour over the remaining coffee, and top with the remaining custard. Tiramisù is one of those puddings where much of its charm lies in its decadent messiness, so don't worry about lining everything up too perfectly. Sprinkle the cocoa generously over the top and refrigerate for at least 1 hour, or until you are ready to serve.

FRIED PUFFS WITH SUGAR

GALANI

MAKES 100 GALANI

4 cups / 500g Italian type "00"
flour or all-purpose flour,
plus more for dusting

1 teaspoon baking powder

A pinch of salt

⅓ cup / 70g granulated sugar

¼ cup (½ stick) / 50g salted butter,
at room temperature

3 large eggs

1 large egg yolk

¼ cup / 30ml grappa or
other eau-de-vie

Peanut oil, for frying

¼ cup / 30g confectioners' sugar,
for dusting

GALANI ARE LIKE PUFFS OF AIR dusted with confectioners' sugar. They are perhaps my favorite among the array of sweet treats that appear in shop windows during the weeks of Carnival, only to vanish again for another year when the holiday draws to an end. While people in Venice may be strict about eating these only during the weeks of Carnival, I see no reason why you shouldn't flout convention and serve them with a pot of coffee after dinner any night of the year. I do. They're bliss.

Sift the flour, baking powder, and salt into a large bowl. Add the granulated sugar and stir everything together with a wooden spoon. Rub the butter into the mixture using your thumb and forefinger until you have something that resembles coarse sand.

Crack the eggs and egg yolk into a small bowl, lightly beat with a fork, then pour the eggs into the flour mixture. Add the grappa and use your hands to bring the dough together, kneading it a little with your hands, until it feels smooth and elastic to the touch. If the dough feels too stiff and crumbly, add a tablespoon or two of water. Roll the dough into a ball, wrap it in plastic wrap, and let it rest at room temperature for 30 minutes.

Divide the dough into 3 equal pieces. On a lightly floured surface, use a rolling pin to roll out the first piece of dough until it is thin enough to fit into the pasta machine. Roll the dough through each setting of the machine until it is the thinnest it can be. If you don't have a pasta machine, just use your rolling pin and roll the dough as thin as you can. Ideally, it would be paper-thin (2 to 3mm)—the finer the pastry, the lighter and more delicate the galani will be. Use a sharp knife to cut the rolled sheet of pastry into rectangles roughly 2 by 4 inches (5 by 10cm) in size, then make 2 slits down the middle of each rectangle. Repeat this same process with the remaining 2 pieces of dough.

Fill a large heavy-bottomed pot or a deep-fryer with enough peanut oil to fill it halfway. Set the pot over high heat until it reaches 325° to 375°F. To test if it's ready, drop a cube of bread in; it should sizzle and turn golden in 30 seconds.

Using a slotted spoon, and working in batches of 2 or 3, gently lower the pieces of pastry into the hot oil. Fry, turning them over halfway, until golden brown, 2 minutes. Lift the galani out of the oil and put them on paper towels to soak up excess oil.

Let cool, then pile the pastries high on a serving dish and cover with a generous sprinkling of confectioners' sugar. (These will keep well in an airtight container for up to 1 week.)

ORANGE BLOSSOM AND ALMOND TART

TORTA DI MANDORLE E FIOR D'ARANCIO

SERVES 8 TO 10

FOR THE PASTRY

2⅓ cups / 300g all-purpose flour, plus more for dusting

⅔ cup / 150g cold salted butter

A pinch of salt

FOR THE FILLING

4 cups / 550g blanched almonds

1 cup / 210g granulated sugar

1 teaspoon orange blossom water

4 large egg whites

¾ cup / 240g good-quality thick-cut orange marmalade

ALMOND TART IS MUCH LOVED in Venice, and most *pasticcerie* sell it both by the slice and in whole tart form. In my version here, I've layered the almond crumble with a sharp orange marmalade, but you could also try a raspberry, fig, or plum jam filling. Or simply make it plain.

Don't be tempted to make this with already ground almonds; they are too fine. You want the filling to be coarse and nutty. Buy whole blanched almonds and process them briefly in a food processor.

Make the pastry. Pulse the flour in a food processor for a few seconds to lightly sift it, then add the butter and process again until the mixture has the consistency of coarse sand. (To make the dough without a food processor, sift the flour into a large bowl and rub in the butter with your fingertips until the mixture has the texture of coarse sand.) Remove the processor blade, stir in the salt, and add 2 to 3 tablespoons of cold water. Transfer the mixture to a clean work surface. Bring the dough together with your hands. Be careful not to overwork the dough, as this will make the pastry tough and chewy rather than light and crisp. Shape the dough into a ball, wrap it in plastic wrap, and refrigerate for at least 30 minutes.

On a lightly floured surface, use a rolling pin to roll out the dough into a disk that is slightly larger in diameter than the base of a 10-inch (27cm) tart pan and ¼ inch (3 to 5mm) thick. Gently lift the dough on the rolling pin and lay it into the tart pan, pressing it down into the nooks and crannies. Pierce the base here and there with a fork, then roll over the top with the rolling pin to cut away excess pastry. Chill for 15 to 20 minutes.

Preheat the oven to 400°F.

Cover the pastry with parchment paper, then fill it with baking beans or weights. Bake for 15 minutes, until dry to the touch, then remove the paper and weights and bake the pastry again until very lightly golden all over, 5 to 7 minutes. Remove from the oven and let cool briefly.

Make the filling. Place the almonds in a food processor and pulse until coarsely ground. Add the sugar and orange blossom water, and pulse again to combine.

In a large, clean bowl, whisk the egg whites until they form stiff peaks, 2 to 3 minutes. Gently fold them into the almond mixture.

Spread the orange marmalade, chunky peel and all, into the pastry shell. Spread the almond filling over the jam.

Bake for 20 to 25 more minutes, until golden all over.

MASCARPONE TART WITH FIGS

CROSTATA DI FICHI
E MASCARPONE

SERVES 8 TO 10

FOR THE PASTRY

1 cup plus 3 tablespoons /
150g all-purpose flour,
plus more for dusting

⅓ cup / 75g cold salted butter,
chopped

A generous pinch of salt

1 cup / 65g confectioners' sugar

2 large egg yolks

FOR THE FILLING

1 large egg

¼ cup / 30g granulated sugar

⅔ cup / 150g mascarpone

12 to 14 fresh figs, peeled,
stemmed, and halved

I LIKE TO THINK OF THIS TART as a blank canvas, which on this occasion I've piled high with luscious figs, but that you could just as well top with whatever fruit is in season: strawberries, raspberries, roasted plums, or, if you want something a little sharper, fresh red currants or rarer saffron-hued cape gooseberries. You could even forget the fruit and top it with shavings of bitter chocolate instead.

Make the pastry. Add the flour, butter, and salt to a food processor. Process until the mixture has the texture of coarse sand. (Or, if you don't have a food processor, then use your fingers to rub the butter into the flour.) Remove the blade, sift in the confectioners' sugar, and add the egg yolks. Transfer the mixture to a clean work surface. Bring the dough together with your hands. You want the dough to feel smooth and pliable, but don't be tempted to overwork it; just bring it together. If it's too dry and crumbly, add a tablespoon or two of cold water. Roll it into a ball, wrap in plastic wrap, and set in the refrigerator for 30 minutes.

On a lightly floured surface, roll out the dough into a large disk about ⅛ inch (3 to 5mm) thick. Using the rolling pin, gently transfer the pastry to a 10-inch (27cm) tart pan, pressing it down into the nooks and crannies. Pierce the base a few times with a fork, and roll the top of the pan with the rolling pin to trim away excess pastry. Chill for a further 15 to 20 minutes.

Preheat the oven to 350°F.

Line the pastry shell with parchment paper and fill it with baking beans or weights. Bake for 10 minutes. Take the pan out of the oven, remove the paper and weights, and bake for 10 to 15 more minutes, until lightly golden brown all over. Let cool.

Make the filling. Separate the egg into 2 medium bowls. Whisk the egg white until frothy, 1 to 2 minutes. Little by little, add half the sugar and keep whisking until it starts to form stiff peaks.

Whisk the yolk and the remaining sugar together until pale and creamy, 2 to 3 minutes. Beat in the mascarpone until you have a smooth cream, 1 to 2 minutes. Gently fold the yolk mixture into the egg whites. Spoon the mixture into the cooled pastry shell, then arrange the figs on top.

PINE NUT AND CUSTARD TART

TORTA DI PINOLI

SERVES 8 TO 10

FOR THE PASTRY

7 tablespoons / 200g salted butter

3 cups plus 3 tablespoons /
400g all-purpose flour,
plus more for dusting

1½ cups / 170g confectioners' sugar

4 large egg yolks

FOR THE FILLING

2 cups / 500ml whole milk

5 large egg yolks

¾ cup / 125g granulated sugar

⅓ cup / 40g all-purpose flour

1 teaspoon vanilla extract

1 cup / 120g pine nuts

ALSO KNOWN AS *TORTA DELLA NONNA,* or "grandmother's cake," this is a sweet my grandmother unfortunately never made for me. I came to savor its delights late in life; but, nonetheless, I am now a great convert. Like any tart that is layered with custard, this is creamy, but because of the pine nuts, which are so rich in texture, it is even creamier than you can quite imagine. And it's not too sweet, either.

Make the pastry. Process the butter and flour in a food processor until you have a mixture the consistency of grainy sand. (If you don't have a food processor, rub the butter into the flour with your thumb and forefinger in a bowl.) Remove the blade, then sift the confectioners' sugar in with the flour and butter. Add the egg yolks, and use your hands to bring the dough together. If it feels to dry and crumbly, add 1 to 2 tablespoons cold water. Roll the dough into a ball, wrap it in plastic wrap, and refrigerate for at least 30 minutes.

Preheat the oven to 400°F.

On a lightly floured work surface, roll out the dough using a rolling pin into a large disk that is roughly ⅛ inch (3 to 5 mm) thick. Gently lift the dough using the rolling pin and lay it into a 10-inch (27cm) tart pan. Gently press it down into the nooks and crannies, then roll over the top of the pan with the rolling pin to cut away excess pastry. Prick the bottom of the tart all over with a fork. Cover the pastry with parchment paper and fill with baking beans or weights.

Bake for 15 minutes, or until dry to the touch, then remove the parchment paper and weights, put the tart shell back in the oven, and bake for 5 to 7 minutes more, or until the pastry is lightly golden. Remove and let cool briefly. Reduce the oven temperature to 350°F.

Make the filling. Add the milk to a medium saucepan set over medium-low heat, and slowly heat until it starts steaming and little bubbles start rising around the edges. Take care not to let it boil.

In a large bowl, whisk the egg yolks and granulated sugar until pale and fluffy. Sift in the flour and slowly, while continuously whisking the eggs, gradually pour in the hot milk. Whisk in the vanilla. Return the mixture to the saucepan over gentle heat and simmer, whisking, until it thickens to a rich custard consistency, 4 to 5 minutes.

Pour the custard into the pastry shell and top with the pine nuts. Bake for 20 to 25 minutes, until golden and just set in the middle. Let cool briefly, then remove the rim of the tart pan. Serve warm.

ZABAIONE AND MERINGUE SEMIFREDDO

SEMIFREDDO DI ZABAIONE E MERINGA

SERVES 10 TO 12

FOR THE MERINGUE

½ lemon

6 large egg whites

1½ cups / 300g granulated sugar

FOR THE ZABAIONE

6 large egg yolks

½ cup / 100g granulated sugar

4½ tablespoons / 70ml Marsala or other sweet wine

1¼ cups / 300ml heavy cream

SHEETS OF WHITE MERINGUE, crisp on the outside and blissfully chewy at their center, layered with a soft, creamy zabaione: this is semifreddo-meets-cake-meets-pavlova. There is something about the pure white-on-whiteness of this that I find seductive, but I won't deny that a handful of tart red berries or some roughly chopped glacéed citrus peel buried in each tier of zabaione holds an equally alluring more-is-more charm about it.

Make the meringue layers first. Preheat the oven to 275°F. Line 3 large baking sheets with parchment paper. Draw 3 circles roughly 9 inches (24cm) in diameter on the paper. (I use a cake pan as my guide.) Turn the paper over so you can still see the lines and use them as guides.

Rub the inside of a clean bowl with half a lemon to remove any traces of grease. Pour the whites into the bowl. Using an electric mixer, beat on medium-low speed until the whites begin to froth, 1 to 2 minutes. Increase the speed to high and begin adding the sugar 1 spoonful at a time, until the whites become glossy and start to form stiff peaks, 2 to 3 minutes. Spoon the meringue onto the baking sheets and use the back of the spoon to spread it out evenly to fill the circles.

Bake for 1 hour 10 minutes. Switch off the oven and leave the meringues in the oven, without opening the door, for 1 more hour, until the oven has cooled. Take the meringues out of the oven and let them cool on the baking sheets. (You can make these a few days ahead and store them in an airtight container, if you like.)

Make the zabaione. Fill a saucepan up to one-third with cold water and bring to a boil. Choose a heatproof bowl that fits snugly over the saucepan, then add the egg yolks and sugar to the bowl. Whisk until light and fluffy, 2 to 3 minutes. As the yolks begin to froth up, set the bowl over the simmering water and keep whisking until a trail, a little like runny honey, forms as you lift the whisk, 5 to 7 minutes. Be very careful that the hot water doesn't touch the bottom of the bowl, as that will cause the yolks to cook. Pour the Marsala into the yolks, little by little, whisking all the while. This should take 3 to 5 minutes, and as you add the liquid, the zabaione will double in size and become as thick as heavy cream. Remove the bowl from the heat and let the zabaione cool to room temperature.

In a second bowl, use an electric mixer to whisk the cream until stiff, 2 to 3 minutes. Gently fold the cream into the cooled zabaione.

Place one meringue on a serving plate, and spoon half the zabaione cream over it. Top with a second meringue, the rest of the zabaione, and then the third meringue. Freeze for 3 to 4 hours to chill and set.

BURNT SUGAR, AMARETTI, AND RICOTTA CAKE

TORTA DI RICOTTA E AMARETTI BRÛLÉE

SERVES 8 TO 10

1 cup / 130g raisins

3 tablespoons / 50ml brandy of choice

⅓ cup / 75g salted butter

45 / 250g amaretti cookies, crumbled

½ lemon

4 large eggs

⅔ cup / 130g granulated sugar

2¼ cups / 500g ricotta

¼ cup / 30g self-rising flour

½ cup / 100g light brown sugar

THIS IS THE SOPHISTICATED "DINNER-PARTY" COUSIN of the breakfast ricotta cake on page 40: a layer of crumbled amaretti cookies, topped with whipped sweet ricotta, peppered with plump brandy-drunken raisins, then gilded with a crust of burnt sugar. It sits halfway between a crème brûlée and a cheesecake, and though it might not be the prettiest of desserts, it is insanely good.

Put the raisins in a small bowl, pour in the brandy, cover with a clean tea towel, and let steep. The longer you leave the raisins to soak up the brandy, the better.

Preheat the oven to 350°F. Line a 9-inch (24cm) cake pan, preferably springform, with parchment paper.

In a small saucepan set over low heat, melt the butter. Add the crumbled amaretti and stir with a wooden spoon. Press the mixture into the bottom of the cake pan.

Bake for 10 minutes, until the bottom crust is firm. Remove the pan from the oven and let cool.

Rub down the inside of a clean mixing bowl with half a lemon. Separate the eggs and add the egg whites to the prepared bowl and the yolks to another mixing bowl. Whisk the egg whites vigorously until they begin to froth, 1 to 2 minutes. Add half of the granulated sugar, little by little and whisking all the while, until they become glossy and stiff, 2 to 3 minutes.

Put the ricotta into the bowl with the egg yolks. I like to work the ricotta through a sieve, which I find gives the cake a silkier texture, but this is optional. Pour in the remaining granulated sugar and stir with a wooden spoon until smooth. Stir in the flour, then fold in the raisins.

Gently fold the beaten egg whites into the ricotta cream, and spread the batter onto the cookie base. Hold the pan in your hands and give it a good jiggle to level out the batter.

Bake for 1 hour, or until a knife comes out clean when inserted in the middle. If the top of the cake is browning too much, cover it with a piece of foil. Remove the pan from the oven and let the cake cool for 5 to 10 minutes. Sprinkle the brown sugar over the top, as evenly as you can, and, if desired, use a kitchen blowtorch or place the pan under the broiler briefly to melt the sugar so that you get patches of burnt, crisp sugar.

Refrigerate the cake for at least 3 hours or overnight before removing it from the pan and serving.

PANETTONE, MASCARPONE, AND ALMOND CAKE

TORTA DI PANETTONE CON
CREMA DI MASCARPONE
E MANDORLE

SERVES 10

1 cup / 250g salted butter,
at room temperature

4 cups / 500g confectioners' sugar

1¼ cups / 320g mascarpone,
at room temperature

1 cup / 100g ground almonds

1 panettone (roughly
2¼ pounds / 1kg)

3 glacéed cherries, for decoration

Small handful of fresh bay leaves,
for decoration

THIS IS WHAT YOU MIGHT CALL gilding the proverbial lily—but then, a lot of that has gone on in Venice over the centuries. In truth, a really good panettone—light and airy, and fresh from the baker—needs nothing done to it and should be eaten as is with a glass of dessert wine (or for breakfast with a mug of hot chocolate; see page 62). More often than not, though, the panettone we buy in boxes from the shops could do with a little extra something.

This is a wonderful way to make use of a slightly stale panettone; you layer it with a thick almond and mascarpone buttercream, then decorate it like a cake. Once iced, the panettone should really be eaten within a day. The mascarpone and butter should both be at room temperature before you start: if the mascarpone is too cold, it will form lumps when it's mixed with the butter.

Beat the butter with an electric mixer at high speed until pale and fluffy, 2 to 3 minutes. Sift in half the confectioners' sugar, and beat until well combined. Pour in the remaining confectioners' sugar and beat until smooth. Then beat in the mascarpone until just combined. Take care not to overbeat, or the cream will become grainy and lumpy. Using a wooden spoon, stir in the ground almonds.

Use a bread knife to slice off the "muffin top" of the panettone to create a level top; discard the trimmings. (If I don't gobble them up there and then, I slice them into small finger pieces and serve them for afternoon tea or breakfast.) Peel away the wrapping around the sides and bottom of the panettone, then cut crosswise through the middle with the bread knife so that you have 2 or 3 tiers of cake. (How many will depend on the height of your panettone; some are a little taller and comfortably allow for 3 layers, while others are more squat and allow for only 2.)

Place the bottom layer on a cake stand or serving dish, and spread a generous dollop of the mascarpone and almond cream on top. Top with the second layer of panettone (and repeat if you are making a 3-layer cake). Spread the last of the cream on top of the panettone and on the sides. Decorate with the glacéed cherries and bay leaves.

MERINGUE AND CHOCOLATE KISSES

BACI IN GONDOLA

MAKES 15 MERINGUE KISSES

½ lemon

6 large egg whites

1½ cups / 300g granulated sugar

1 cup / 150g chopped dark chocolate

MERINGUES SANDWICHED TOGETHER WITH DARK CHOCOLATE—you will see these in various delightful manifestations, piled high in the windows at *pasticcerie* across town. We call them *baci in gondola*, which translates literally to "kisses upon a gondola," and there is indeed something at once romantic and indulgent about these treats. I like to make mine overblown and messy, rather than delicate like the ones you see in the shops. But then, as you will have gathered, I am a firm believer in homemade sweets looking homemade.

This recipe for meringue, which I have tried and tested in my own kitchen again and again, will give you meringues that are crisp on the outside and a little gooey, almost like marshmallow, on the inside. If you prefer them crisp and dry all the way through, increase your cooking time by a further 10 minutes.

Preheat the oven to 275°F. Line 2 large baking sheets with parchment paper. Draw 15 circles, each roughly 2 inches (5cm) in diameter, on each sheet, allowing plenty of space between them. Turn the paper over so the pen won't transfer onto the meringues but you can still see the lines and use them as a template for the meringues.

Rub the lemon over the inside of a mixing bowl to remove any traces of grease. Pour the egg whites into the bowl, and using an electric hand mixer, beat on medium-low speed until the whites begin to froth, 1 to 2 minutes. Increase the speed to high and begin adding the sugar a spoonful at a time until the whites become glossy and begin to form stiff peaks, 3 to 4 minutes. For slightly neater looking meringues, use a piping bag; if you don't have a piping bag, then just spoon dollops onto the baking sheets using 2 spoons to loosely shape them.

Set the sheets on the upper and lower racks of the oven and bake for 1 hour. Halfway through the cooking time, switch the two sheets, moving as quickly as you can so as not to let too much heat out of the oven. Switch the oven off and leave the meringues in there, without opening the door, for 1 more hour, until the oven has cooled. Take the meringues out of the oven and leave them to cool on the baking sheets.

Fill a saucepan up to one-third full with water and bring to a boil. Choose a heatproof bowl that fits snugly over the saucepan without touching the water, then add the chocolate pieces to the bowl. Heat the chocolate, stirring occasionally, until melted, 3 to 5 minutes. Remove the bowl from the heat. Alternatively, melt the chocolate in a microwave:

recipe continues

break it into small pieces and set the oven on the lowest power possible; melt the chocolate little by little, taking time to give it a stir after each heating interval.

Grasp a meringue by the tip and dip its fat little bottom into the chocolate. Sandwich it with a second meringue. Gently lay the meringue sandwich on one side to let the chocolate cool and set. (If it's a very warm day or you want to speed up the setting process, then pop the meringues in the refrigerator for 5 to 10 minutes.) Continue to assemble the meringue sandwiches. They are best eaten sooner rather than later, though they should keep in an airtight container for 2 to 3 days.

CHOCOLATE BIRTHDAY CAKE

TORTA DI COMPLEANNO

SERVES 12 TO 15

FOR THE CAKE

3½ cups / 600g chopped dark chocolate (about 1½ pounds)

2⅔ cups / 600g salted butter, chopped (about 1½ pounds)

½ lemon

12 large eggs

3 cups / 600g granulated sugar

FOR THE ICING

1⅓ cups / 300g salted butter, at room temperature

3¾ cups / 450g confectioners' sugar

2 cups / 500g mascarpone, at room temperature

MY MOTHER HAS MADE THIS CHOCOLATE CAKE for my birthday every year for as long as I can remember. Now I make it for my son's and my husband's birthdays—and any other days we might want to celebrate along the way. It's a flourless cake, so it is rich and dense, halfway between a mousse and a slab of fudge. When my mother used to make this for me as a child, she would smother it with chocolate buttercream icing and decorate it all over with rainbow-colored sprinkles. I remember distinctly believing there to be nothing more beautiful. Since then, my tastes have become a little more subtle: a layer of white mascarpone icing and a smattering of fresh summer berries or flowers from the garden are usually my go-to embellishments.

You will find that the cake rises hugely in the oven and will then fall back when you take it out. Don't worry if it looks ugly and messy; patch it up with a little icing and serve it as is. It tastes so good that you won't mind that it looks more than a little homemade. This cake keeps very well in the fridge; in fact, its flavor improves with age, so you can make it up to five days ahead of when you plan on eating it, then ice and decorate it a few hours before serving.

Preheat the oven to 340°F. Line two 9-inch (24cm) cake pans, preferably springform, with parchment paper. Place the oven rack in the center of the oven and remove the rack above.

Fill a saucepan up to one-third full with cold water and bring to a boil. Choose a heatproof bowl that fits snugly over the saucepan, and add the chocolate and butter. Set the bowl over the boiling water and heat, stirring every now and then, until the chocolate and the butter have melted, 3 to 4 minutes. Let cool. (Alternatively, melt the chocolate and butter in a microwave: break the chocolate into small pieces and set the microwave oven on the lowest power possible; melt the mixture little by little, taking time to give it a stir after each heating interval.)

Rub the lemon over the inside of a large mixing bowl. Separate the eggs and add the egg whites to the prepared bowl and the yolks to another large mixing bowl. Using an electric mixer, beat the whites on medium-low speed until they begin to froth, 1 to 2 minutes. Increase the speed to high and begin adding the sugar 1 spoonful at a time until the whites become glossy and start to form stiff peaks and you've used up half of the sugar, 2 to 3 minutes.

recipe continues

Whisk the yolks and the remaining sugar until pale and creamy, 2 to 3 minutes. Gently fold in first the egg whites and then the melted chocolate. Divide the batter between the prepared cake pans and smooth the tops.

Bake the layers for 1 hour 20 minutes, or until the tops of the cakes feel firm to the touch. The best way to test if the cakes are done is to hold a pan in your hands and give it a gentle jiggle; the cake should feel solid and not wobble. Set the cakes back in the oven, switch off the heat, and leave them there for 1 to 2 hours, until the oven has cooled. You will notice that the cakes sink back on themselves by about a third—don't worry, that is entirely normal. When the cakes cool to room temperature, refrigerate them for 2 to 3 hours, and ideally overnight, before taking them out of their pans or they will collapse.

Make the icing. Beat the butter until light and fluffy, 2 to 3 minutes. Sift in half the confectioners' sugar and beat well. Sift in the remaining sugar and beat until light and smooth. Use a wooden spoon to stir in the mascarpone.

Carefully take the first cake out of the pan, peel away the paper, and place the cake on a serving plate or cake stand. Use a large bread knife to even out the top so that it is level. Spread half the mascarpone icing on top. Place the second cake on top and level it out by cutting away any excess with a bread knife. Spread the remaining mascarpone icing over the top of the cake, and decorate as you like, with fresh flowers (my particular favorite) or berries.

ACKNOWLEDGMENTS

To my husband, Anthony—for greedily and cheerfully devouring the food I cook, and for always inspiring me to chase after my dreams. You are my everything.

To my Mama—for ignoring the chaos in the kitchen and for cheering me on tirelessly as this book came together.

To Wendy—for teaching me not just how to cook, but how to love to cook.

To Charlie and Ed—for believing in me.

To Doris—for your warmth, generosity, and patience in bringing this book about. To Amanda and Ashley—for helping me find the words to tell the story I had long dreamed of telling. To Marysarah—for bringing this book to life with your beautiful design. And to Carly and Natasha—for making it such fun to work together.

To Dalim and Anna—for all your help in the kitchen. Without you, this book wouldn't exist.

To Poppy—for your help magicking my scribbles and notes into recipes.

To Jo—for being endlessly generous with your time, your wise advice, and above all, your thoughtful encouragement.

To Caroline—for helping me to make sense of my own thoughts, and for patiently casting your stylish eye over each and every iteration of this book, from rough notes to first draft to the real thing.

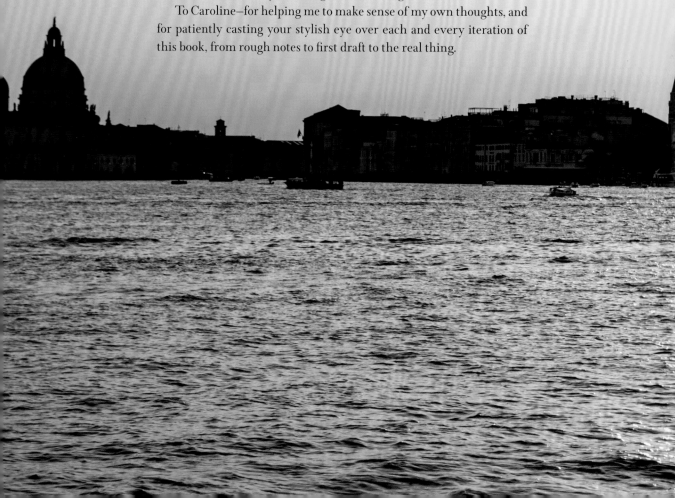

INDEX

Note: Page references in *italics* indicate photographs.

A

Almond(s)
and Figs, Oven-Roasted Porgy with, *224, 225*
and Garden Pea Salad, *94, 95*
and Orange Blossom Tart, *260, 261*
Panettone, and Mascarpone Cake, *272, 273*
Paste Croissants, *32, 33*
Amaretti
about, 17
Burnt Sugar, and Ricotta Cake, *270, 271*
Chocolate and Amaretto Custard, *254, 255*
and Pumpkin Filling, Ravioli with, 144
Amaretto biscuits. *See* Amaretti
Amaretto Syrup, Peaches Poached in, *244, 246*
Anchovies
about, 17
Bigoli in Salsa, 18
and Boiled Eggs, *186, 187*
Sliced Veal in Creamy Tuna and Caper Sauce, *164, 165*
Slow-Cooked Peppers, *98, 99*
Appetizers
Boiled Eggs and Anchovies, *186, 187*
Deep-Fried Risotto and Mozzarella Balls, *180, 181*
Deep-Fried Sage Leaves, *182, 183*
Layered Gorgonzola, Pear, Mascarpone, and Walnut Log, *194, 195*
Poppyseed Puffs, *176, 177*
Three Kinds of Crostini, *190, 191*–92, *193*
Three Prosecco Cocktails, *196, 197*–98
Toasted Ham and Cheese Sandwich, *188, 189*
Walnut Croquettes, *178, 179*
Zucchini, Pecorino, and Fresh Mint Frittata, *184, 185*
Zucchini Pizzette, *174, 175*
Apple(s)
Honey, and Walnut Cake, *42, 43*
Meat, and Sage Skewers, 233
Pears, and Chestnuts, Roast Duck with, *234, 235*
Raisin, Pine Nut, and Cinnamon Bread Pudding, *44–46, 45*
Apricot
Brioche, 26, *27–28*
Jam Daisy Cookies, *58, 59*
and Raisin Sticky Pastries, 36, 38
Artichoke
Fava Bean, Farro, and Mint Salad, *152, 153*
Hearts, Pan-Fried, with Parsley, *74, 75*
Puff Pastry Pie, 104–5, *106*
Asparagus
and Prosecco, Linguine with, *120, 121*
White, with Zabaione Sauce, *108, 109*

B

Bacon. *See* Pancetta
Bean(s)
Butter, with Sage, *92, 93*
Fava, Artichoke, Farro, and Mint Salad, *152, 153*
Beef
Spiced Meatballs, *166, 167*
Bellini, *198, 199*
Bread Pudding, Apple, Raisin, Pine Nut, and Cinnamon, *44–46, 45*
Breads
Apricot Brioche, 26, *27–28*
Chocolate, Orange, and Hazelnut Breakfast, *47–48, 49*
Olive Focaccia, *72, 73*
Sugar Buns, *56, 57*
Breakfast recipes
Almond Paste Croissants, *32, 33*
Apple, Honey, and Walnut Cake, *42, 43*
Apple, Raisin, Pine Nut, and Cinnamon Bread Pudding, *44–46, 45*
Apricot and Raisin Sticky Pastries, 36, 38
Apricot Brioche, 26, *27–28*
Cardamom and Cinnamon Rice Pudding Tartlets, *30–31, 31*
Chocolate, Orange, and Hazelnut Breakfast Bread, *47–48, 49*
Chocolate and Orange Ricotta Breakfast Cake, *40–41, 41*
Fennel Seed and Candied-Peel Yogurt Cake, *50, 51*
Fig and Mascarpone Cake, *52, 53*
Jam Daisy Cookies, *58, 59*
Peach and Saffron Pastries, *34, 35*
Peach Iced Tea, *64, 65*
Polenta and Raisin Cookies, *60, 61*
Sugar Buns, *56, 57*
Thick Hot Chocolate with Zabaione, *62, 63*
Brioche, Apricot, 26, *27–28*
Broth
Chicken, with Tortellini, *128, 129*
for recipes, 20
Shrimp, *214, 215*
vegetable, preparing, 20
Buns, Sugar, *56, 57*
Burrata and Pomegranate, Crostini with, *190, 191*

C

Cakes
Apple, Honey, and Walnut, *42, 43*
Burnt Sugar, Amaretti, and Ricotta, *270, 271*
Chocolate and Orange Ricotta Breakfast, *40–41, 41*
Chocolate Birthday, *277–79, 278*
Fennel Seed and Candied-Peel Yogurt, *50, 51*
Fig and Mascarpone, *52, 53*

Panettone, Mascarpone, and
Almond, *272, 273*
Candied Peel
about, *17*
Apple, Raisin, Pine Nut, and
Cinnamon Bread Pudding,
44–46, *45*
Apricot and Raisin Sticky Pastries,
36, *38*
and Fennel Seed Yogurt Cake,
50, *51*
Raisin and Pine Nut Sugar
Doughnuts with Whipped
Ricotta Cream, 247–49, *248*
Caper and Tuna Sauce, Creamy, Sliced
Veal in, *164, 165*
Cardamom and Cinnamon Rice
Pudding Tartlets, 30–31, *31*
Celery, Roasted, with Cherry
Tomatoes and Pancetta,
80, *81*
Cheese. *See also* Mascarpone;
Parmesan; Ricotta
Artichoke Puff Pastry Pie, 104–5,
106
Baked Polenta with Melted
Gorgonzola, 150, *151*
Crostini with Burrata and
Pomegranate, *190, 191*
Deep-Fried Risotto and Mozzarella
Balls, 180, *181*
and Ham Sandwich, Toasted, 188,
189
Layered Gorgonzola, Pear,
Mascarpone, and Walnut Log,
194, 195
Risotto with Radicchio and
Gorgonzola, 160, *161*
types of, 17–18
Zucchini, Bacon, and Pecorino
Tart, 100, *101*
Zucchini, Pecorino, and Fresh Mint
Frittata, 184, *185*
Zucchini Pizzette, *174, 175*
Chestnuts, Apples, and Pears, Roast
Duck with, 234, *235*
Chicken
Broth with Tortellini, 128, *129*
Meat, Sage, and Apple Skewers, 233
stock, buying, 20
in Tomato and White Wine Sauce,
162, *163*
Chocolate
and Amaretto Custard, 254, *255*

Birthday Cake, 277–79, *278*
buying, 18
and Meringue Kisses, 274, 275–76
Orange, and Hazelnut Breakfast
Bread, 47–48, *49*
and Orange Ricotta Breakfast Cake,
40–41, *41*
Thick Hot, with Zabaione, 62, *63*
Cinnamon and Cardamom Rice
Pudding Tartlets, 30–31, *31*
Citrus peel, candied. *See* Candied
peel
Clams in White Wine Sauce, 210, *211*
Cocktails, Three Prosecco, *196,
197–98*
Coffee
Maria's Famous Tiramisù, 256,
257
Cookies
Jam Daisy, 58, *59*
Meringue and Chocolate Kisses,
274, 275–76
Polenta and Raisin, 60, *61*
Crab and Cherry Tomatoes, Gnocchi
with, 138, *139*
Croissants, Almond Paste, 32, *33*
Croquettes, Walnut, *178, 179*
Crostini
with Burrata and Pomegranate,
190, 191
with Mortadella and Pistachios, 192
with Ricotta, Honey, and Figs, 192,
193
Custard
Chocolate and Amaretto, 254, *255*
and Pine Nut Tart, 266, *267*

D
Desserts
Burnt Sugar, Amaretti, and Ricotta
Cake, 270, *271*
Chocolate and Amaretto Custard,
254, *255*
Chocolate Birthday Cake, 277–79,
278
Fried Puffs with Sugar, 258, *259*
Maria's Famous Tiramisù, 256,
257
Mascarpone Tart with Figs, 263,
265
Meringue and Chocolate Kisses,
274, 275–76
Orange Blossom and Almond Tart,
260, *261*

Panettone, Mascarpone, and
Almond Cake, *272, 273*
Peaches Poached in Amaretto
Syrup, 244, *246*
Pine Nut and Custard Tart, 266,
267
Raisin and Pine Nut Sugar
Doughnuts with Whipped
Ricotta Cream, 247–49, *248*
Saffron Panna Cotta, 252, *253*
Strawberry and Vodka Sorbet, 250,
251
Zabaione and Meringue
Semifreddo, 268, *269*
Doughnuts, Raisin and Pine Nut Sugar,
with Whipped Ricotta Cream,
247–49, *248*
Drinks
Peach Iced Tea, 64, *65*
Thick Hot Chocolate with
Zabaione, 62, *63*
Three Prosecco Cocktails, *196,
197–98*
Duck
Legs, Roasted, with Plums, 236,
237
Roast, with Apples, Pears, and
Chestnuts, 234, *235*

E
Eggs
Boiled, and Anchovies, 186, *187*
Zucchini, Pecorino, and Fresh Mint
Frittata, 184, *185*

F
Farro, Artichoke, Fava Bean, and Mint
Salad, 152, *153*
Fennel
Gratin of, 90, *91*
Risotto, 158, *159*
Fennel Seed and Candied-Peel Yogurt
Cake, 50, *51*
Fig(s)
and Almonds, Oven-Roasted Porgy
with, 224, *225*
Apple, Raisin, Pine Nut, and
Cinnamon Bread Pudding,
44–46, *45*
and Langoustine Salad, 216, *217*
and Mascarpone Cake, 52, *53*
Mascarpone Tart with, 263, *265*
Ricotta, and Honey, Crostini with,
192, *193*

Fish. *See also* Anchovies
　　Oven-Roasted Porgy with Almonds
　　　　and Figs, *224, 225*
　　Oven-Roasted Stuffed Sardines,
　　　　220, 221
　　Oven-Roasted Turbot with
　　　　Potatoes, Olives, and Cherry
　　　　Tomatoes, *231, 232*
　　Salt-Baked Sea Bass, *228, 229*
　　Sliced Veal in Creamy Tuna and
　　　　Caper Sauce, *164, 165*
　　Sole in Saffron Sauce, *226, 227*
Flour
　　all-purpose, about, *18*
　　bread, about, *18*
　　Italian-type "00," about, *18*
　　self-rising, making your own, *18*
Focaccia Bread, Olive, *72, 73*
Frittata, Zucchini, Pecorino, and Fresh
　　Mint, *184, 185*
Fruit. *See specific fruits*

G

Gnocchi
　　with Cherry Tomatoes and Crab,
　　　　138, 139
　　Homemade, with Butter and Sage,
　　　　133–35, 134
Gorgonzola
　　Melted, Baked Polenta with, *150, 151*
　　Pear, Mascarpone, and Walnut Log,
　　　　Layered, *194, 195*
　　and Radicchio, Risotto with, *160,*
　　　　161
Gratin of Fennel, *90, 91*

H

Ham. *See* Prosciutto
Hazelnut, Chocolate, and Orange
　　Breakfast Bread, *47–48, 49*
Herbs. *See also specific herbs*
　　about, *18*
　　growing, *18*
Honey
　　Apple, and Walnut Cake, *42, 43*
　　Ricotta, and Figs, Crostini with,
　　　　192, 193

I

Iced Tea, Peach, *64, 65*

J

Jam Daisy Cookies, *58, 59*

K

Kisses, Meringue and Chocolate, *274,*
　　275-76

L

Langoustine(s)
　　and Fig Salad, *216, 217*
　　Poached, with Saffron Mayonnaise,
　　　　212, 213
Lasagna, Pheasant and Radicchio, *146,*
　　147–48
Lemon
　　and Ricotta Filling, Ravioli with, *143*
　　Risotto, *154, 155*
Lobster, Spaghetti with, *131, 132*
Lunch dishes
　　Artichoke, Fava Bean, Farro, and
　　　　Mint Salad, *152, 153*
　　Baked Polenta with Melted
　　　　Gorgonzola, *150, 151*
　　Bigoli with Creamy Walnut Sauce,
　　　　122–24, 123
　　Chicken Broth with Tortellini,
　　　　128, 129
　　Chicken in Tomato and White
　　　　Wine Sauce, *162, 163*
　　Fennel Risotto, *158, 159*
　　Garden Pea and Pancetta Risotto,
　　　　156, 157
　　Gnocchi with Cherry Tomatoes
　　　　and Crab, *138, 139*
　　Homemade Gnocchi with Butter
　　　　and Sage, *133–35, 134*
　　Lemon Risotto, *154, 155*
　　Linguine with Asparagus and
　　　　Prosecco, *120, 121*
　　Pheasant and Radicchio Lasagna,
　　　　146, 147–48
　　Risotto with Radicchio and
　　　　Gorgonzola, *160, 161*
　　Sliced Veal in Creamy Tuna and
　　　　Caper Sauce, *164, 165*
　　Spaghetti with Lobster, *131, 132*
　　Spiced Meatballs, *166, 167*
　　Tagliolini with Shrimp, Zucchini,
　　　　and Saffron, *125, 126–27*
　　Three Kinds of Ravioli, *141–44,*
　　　　142

M

Main courses
　　Baked Mussels with Bread Crumbs
　　　　and Lemon, *206, 207*
　　Bigoli in Salsa, *18*

Clams in White Wine Sauce, *210,*
　　211
Meat, Sage, and Apple Skewers,
　　233
Oven-Roasted Porgy with Almonds
　　and Figs, *224, 225*
Oven-Roasted Stuffed Sardines,
　　220, 221
Oven-Roasted Turbot with
　　Potatoes, Olives, and Cherry
　　Tomatoes, *231, 232*
Poached Langoustines with Saffron
　　Mayonnaise, *212, 213*
Roast Duck with Apples, Pears, and
　　Chestnuts, *234, 235*
Roasted Duck Legs with Plums,
　　236, 237
Sage and Butter Roasted Pheasant,
　　238, 239
Salt-Baked Sea Bass, *228, 229*
Shrimp Broth, *214, 215*
Sole in Saffron Sauce, *226, 227*
Mascarpone
　　about, *18*
　　Chocolate Birthday Cake, *277–79,*
　　　　278
　　and Fig Cake, *52, 53*
　　Gorgonzola, Pear, and Walnut Log,
　　　　Layered, *194, 195*
　　Maria's Famous Tiramisù, *256, 257*
　　Panettone, and Almond Cake, *272,*
　　　　273
　　Ricotta, and Speck Filling, Ravioli
　　　　with, *143*
　　Tart with Figs, *263, 265*
Mayonnaise, Saffron, Poached
　　Langoustines with, *212, 213*
Meat. *See* Beef; Pork; Veal
Meatballs, Spiced, *166, 167*
Meringue
　　and Chocolate Kisses, *274, 275–76*
　　and Zabaione Semifreddo, *268,*
　　　　269
Mint
　　Artichoke, Fava Bean, and Farro
　　　　Salad, *152, 153*
　　Fresh, Zucchini, and Pecorino
　　　　Frittata, *184, 185*
　　and Ricotta–Stuffed Zucchini
　　　　Flowers, *88, 89*
　　Spinach, and Ricotta Pie, *111–13,*
　　　　112
Mortadella and Pistachios, Crostini
　　with, *192*

Mozzarella
about, 17–18
and Risotto Balls, Deep-Fried, 180
Zucchini Pizzette, *174*, 175
Mussels, Baked, with Bread Crumbs
and Lemon, 206, 207

N

Nuts. *See also* Almond(s); Pine Nut(s);
Walnut
Chocolate, Orange, and Hazelnut
Breakfast Bread, 47–48, *49*
Crostini with Mortadella and
Pistachios, 192
Roast Duck with Apples, Pears, and
Chestnuts, 234, 235
Scallops on the Shell with Pistachio
Gratin, 208, 209

O

Olive oil, buying, 18–19
Olive(s)
Focaccia Bread, 72, 73
Oven-Roasted Porgy with Almonds
and Figs, 224, 225
Potatoes, and Cherry Tomatoes,
Oven-Roasted Turbot with,
231, 232
Onions
Bigoli in Salsa, 18
Nonna's Peas, 84, 85
Raisins, and Pine Nuts, Roasted
Pumpkin with, 96, 97
Orange
Chocolate, and Hazelnut Breakfast
Bread, 47–48, *49*
and Chocolate Ricotta Breakfast
Cake, 40–41, *41*
Orange Blossom and Almond Tart,
260, 261

P

Pancetta
and Cherry Tomatoes, Roasted
Celery with, 80, 81
and Garden Pea Risotto, 156, 157
Meat, Sage, and Apple Skewers, 233
Pheasant and Radicchio Lasagna,
146, 147–48
Zucchini, Bacon, and Pecorino
Tart, 100, *101*
Panettone, Mascarpone, and Almond
Cake, 272, 273

Panna Cotta, Saffron, 252, 253
Pantry items, 17–20
Parmesan
about, 17
Artichoke Puff Pastry Pie, 104–5,
106
Bigoli with Creamy Walnut Sauce,
122–24, *123*
Fennel Risotto, 158, *159*
Garden Pea and Pancetta Risotto,
156, 157
Gnocchi with Cherry Tomatoes
and Crab, 138, *139*
Gratin of Fennel, 90, 91
Homemade Gnocchi with Butter
and Sage, 133–35, *134*
Lemon Risotto, *154*, 155
Linguine with Asparagus and
Prosecco, *120*, 121
Pheasant and Radicchio Lasagna,
146, 147–48
Ravioli with Pumpkin and
Amaretti Filling, 144
Risotto with Radicchio and
Gorgonzola, *160*, 161
Parsley
Garden Pea and Almond Salad,
94, 95
Pan-Fried Artichoke Hearts with,
74, 75
Pasta
Bigoli in Salsa, 18
Bigoli with Creamy Walnut Sauce,
122–24, *123*
Chicken Broth with Tortellini,
128, *129*
dried, buying, 19
Gnocchi with Cherry Tomatoes
and Crab, 138, *139*
Homemade Gnocchi with Butter
and Sage, 133–35, *134*
Linguine with Asparagus and
Prosecco, *120*, 121
pairing with sauces, 19
Pheasant and Radicchio Lasagna,
146, 147–48
Spaghetti with Lobster, *131*, 132
Tagliolini with Shrimp, Zucchini,
and Saffron, 125, *126–27*
Three Kinds of Ravioli, 141–44, *142*
Pastries
Almond Paste Croissants, 32, 33
Apricot and Raisin Sticky, 36, 38
Peach and Saffron, 34, 35

Peach(es)
Bellini, 198, *199*
Iced Tea, *64*, 65
Poached in Amaretto Syrup, 244,
246
and Saffron Pastries, 34, 35
Pear(s)
Apple, Raisin, Pine Nut, and
Cinnamon Bread Pudding,
44–46, *45*
Apples, and Chestnuts, Roast Duck
with, 234, 235
Gorgonzola, Mascarpone, and
Walnut Log, Layered, *194*, 195
Pea(s)
Garden, and Almond Salad, 94, 95
Garden, and Pancetta Risotto, 156,
157
Nonna's, 84, 85
Pecorino
Artichoke Puff Pastry Pie, 104–5,
106
Zucchini, and Bacon Tart, 100,
101
Zucchini Pizzette, *174*, 175
Peppers, Slow-Cooked, 98, 99
Pheasant
and Radicchio Lasagna, *146*, 147–48
Sage and Butter Roasted, 238, 239
Pies
Artichoke Puff Pastry, 104–5, *106*
Spinach, Ricotta, and Mint, 111–13,
112
Pine Nut(s)
about, 19
Apple, Raisin, and Cinnamon
Bread Pudding, 44–46, *45*
and Custard Tart, 266, 267
Italian, buying, 19
Onions, and Raisins, Roasted
Pumpkin with, 96, 97
Oven-Roasted Stuffed Sardines,
220, *221*
and Raisins, Spinach with, 78, 79
and Raisin Sugar Doughnuts
with Whipped Ricotta Cream,
247–49, *248*
Pistachio(s)
Gratin, Scallops on the Shell with,
208, 209
and Mortadella, Crostini with, 192
Pizzette, Zucchini, *174*, 175
Plums, Roasted Duck Legs with, 236,
237

Polenta
  about, 19
  Baked, with Melted Gorgonzola,
    150, 151
  and Raisin Cookies, 60, 61
Pomegranate
  and Burrata, Crostini with, 190, 191
  Roasted Radicchio with, 102, 103
Poppyseed Puffs, 176, 177
Porgy, Oven-Roasted, with Almonds
    and Figs, 224, 225
Pork. See also Pancetta; Prosciutto
  Chicken Broth with Tortellini,
    128, 129
  Crostini with Mortadella and
    Pistachios, 192
  Meat, Sage, and Apple Skewers, 233
  Ravioli with Mascarpone, Ricotta,
    and Speck Filling, 143
Potatoes
  Artichoke Puff Pastry Pie, 104–5,
    106
  Homemade Gnocchi with Butter
    and Sage, 133–35, 134
  Olives, and Cherry Tomatoes,
    Oven-Roasted Turbot with,
    231, 232
  Shrimp and Chips, 218, 219
  Walnut Croquettes, 178, 179
Poultry and game birds. See Chicken;
    Duck; Pheasant
Prosciutto
  Toasted Ham and Cheese
    Sandwich, 188, 189
Prosecco
  about, 19
  and Asparagus, Linguine with,
    120, 121
  Cocktails, Three, 196, 197–98
  Strawberry and Vodka Sorbet, 250,
    251
  White Asparagus with Zabaione
    Sauce, 108, 109
Puff Pastry
  Almond Paste Croissants, 32, 33
  Apricot and Raisin Sticky Pastries,
    36, 38
  buying, 19
  Peach and Saffron Pastries, 34, 35
  Pie, Artichoke, 104–5, 106
  Poppyseed Puffs, 176, 177
  Zucchini, Bacon, and Pecorino
    Tart, 100, 101
  Zucchini Pizzette, 174, 175

Puffs, Fried, with Sugar, 258, 259
Pumpkin
  and Amaretti Filling, Ravioli with,
    144
  Roasted, with Onions, Raisins, and
    Pine Nuts, 96, 97
  Soup, Cream of, 86, 87

R
Radicchio
  and Gorgonzola, Risotto with, 160,
    161
  and Pheasant Lasagna, 146, 147–48
  Roasted, with Pomegranate, 102,
    103
Raisin(s)
  about, 19
  Apple, Pine Nut, and Cinnamon
    Bread Pudding, 44–46, 45
  and Apricot Sticky Pastries, 36, 38
  Burnt Sugar, Amaretti, and Ricotta
    Cake, 270, 271
  Chocolate, Orange, and Hazelnut
    Breakfast Bread, 47–48, 49
  Onions, and Pine Nuts, Roasted
    Pumpkin with, 96, 97
  and Pine Nuts, Spinach with,
    78, 79
  and Pine Nut Sugar Doughnuts
    with Whipped Ricotta Cream,
    247–49, 248
  and Polenta Cookies, 60, 61
Ravioli
  with Mascarpone, Ricotta, and
    Speck Filling, 143
  with Pumpkin and Amaretti
    Filling, 144
  recipe for, 141, 142
  with Ricotta and Lemon Filling,
    143
Rice. See also Risotto
  Pudding Tartlets, Cardamom and
    Cinnamon, 30–31, 31
Ricotta
  about, 18
  Breakfast Cake, Chocolate and
    Orange, 40–41, 41
  Burnt Sugar, and Amaretti Cake,
    270, 271
  Cream, Whipped, Raisin and Pine
    Nut Sugar Doughnuts with,
    247–49, 248
  Honey, and Figs, Crostini with,
    192, 193

Layered Gorgonzola, Pear,
    Mascarpone, and Walnut Log,
    194, 195
  and Lemon Filling, Ravioli with,
    143
  making your own, 18
  Mascarpone, and Speck Filling,
    Ravioli with, 143
  and Mint–Stuffed Zucchini
    Flowers, 88, 89
  Spinach, and Mint Pie, 111–13, 112
Risotto
  choosing rice for, 19–20
  Fennel, 158, 159
  Garden Pea and Pancetta, 156, 157
  Lemon, 154, 155
  and Mozzarella Balls, Deep-Fried,
    180, 181
  with Radicchio and Gorgonzola,
    160, 161
Rossini, 198, 199

S
Saffron
  about, 20
  cooking with, 20
  Mayonnaise, Poached Langoustines
    with, 212, 213
  Panna Cotta, 252, 253
  and Peach Pastries, 34, 35
  Sauce, Sole in, 226, 227
  Shrimp, and Zucchini, Tagliolini
    with, 125, 126–27
Sage
  and Butter, Homemade Gnocchi
    with, 133–35, 134
  Butter Beans with, 92, 93
  and Butter Roasted Pheasant, 238,
    239
  Leaves, Deep-Fried, 182, 183
  Meat, and Apple Skewers, 233
Salads
  Artichoke, Fava Bean, Farro, and
    Mint, 152, 153
  Garden Pea and Almond, 94, 95
  Langoustine and Fig, 216, 217
Salt, for recipes, 20
Salt-Baked Sea Bass, 228, 229
Sandwich, Toasted Ham and Cheese,
    188, 189
Sardines, Oven-Roasted Stuffed, 220,
    221
Scallops on the Shell with Pistachio
    Gratin, 208, 209

Sea Bass, Salt-Baked s, *228*, *229*
Semifreddo, Zabaione and Meringue, *268*, *269*
Shellfish
   Baked Mussels with Bread Crumbs and Lemon, *206*, *207*
   Clams in White Wine Sauce, *210*, *211*
   Gnocchi with Cherry Tomatoes and Crab, *138*, *139*
   Langoustine and Fig Salad, *216*, *217*
   Poached Langoustines with Saffron Mayonnaise, *212*, *213*
   Scallops on the Shell with Pistachio Gratin, *208*, *209*
   Shrimp and Chips, *218*, *219*
   Shrimp Broth, *214*, *215*
   Spaghetti with Lobster, *131*, *132*
   Tagliolini with Shrimp, Zucchini, and Saffron, *125*, *126–27*
Shrimp
   Broth, *214*, *215*
   and Chips, *218*, *219*
   Zucchini, and Saffron, Tagliolini with, *125*, *126–27*
Sole in Saffron Sauce, *226*, *227*
Sorbet, Strawberry and Vodka, *250*, *251*
Soups
   Chicken Broth with Tortellini, *128*, *129*
   Cream of Pumpkin, *86*, *87*
Speck, Mascarpone, and Ricotta Filling, Ravioli with, *143*
Spices, for recipes, *20*
Spinach
   with Pine Nuts and Raisins, *78*, *79*
   Ricotta, and Mint Pie, *111–13*, *112*
Spritz, *196*, *197*
Squash. *See also* Zucchini
   Cream of Pumpkin Soup, *86*, *87*
   Ravioli with Pumpkin and Amaretti Filling, *144*
   Roasted Pumpkin with Onions, Raisins, and Pine Nuts, *96*, *97*
Starters
   Baked Mussels with Bread Crumbs and Lemon, *206*, *207*
   Langoustine and Fig Salad, *216*, *217*
   Scallops on the Shell with Pistachio Gratin, *208*, *209*
   Shrimp and Chips, *218*, *219*

Stocks
   chicken or meat, buying, *20*
   for recipes, *20*
Strawberry(ies)
   Rossini, *198*, *199*
   and Vodka Sorbet, *250*, *251*
Sugar Buns, *56*, *57*

T
Taleggio
   about, *18*
   Toasted Ham and Cheese Sandwich, *188*, *189*
Tartlets, Cardamom and Cinnamon Rice Pudding, *30–31*, *31*
Tarts
   Mascarpone, with Figs, *263*, *265*
   Orange Blossom and Almond, *260*, *261*
   Pine Nut and Custard, *266*, *267*
   Zucchini, Bacon, and Pecorino, *100*, *101*
Tea, Peach Iced, *64*, *65*
Tiramisù, Maria's Famous, *256*, *257*
Tomato(es)
   Cherry, and Crab, Gnocchi with, *138*, *139*
   Cherry, and Pancetta, Roasted Celery with, *80*, *81*
   Cherry, Potatoes, and Olives, Oven-Roasted Turbot with, *231*, *232*
   Slow-Cooked Peppers, *98*, *99*
   Spaghetti with Lobster, *131*, *132*
   and White Wine Sauce, Chicken in, *162*, *163*
   Zucchini Pizzette, *174*, *175*
Tuna and Caper Sauce, Creamy, Sliced Veal in, *164*, *165*
Turbot, Oven-Roasted, with Potatoes, Olives, and Cherry Tomatoes, *231*, *232*

V
Veal, Sliced, in Creamy Tuna and Caper Sauce, *164*, *165*
Vegetable(s). *See also specific vegetables*
   broth, preparing, *20*
Vodka and Strawberry Sorbet, *250*, *251*

W
Walnut
   Apple, and Honey Cake, *42*, *43*
   Croquettes, *178*, *179*

Gorgonzola, Pear, and Mascarpone Log, Layered, *194*, *195*
Sauce, Creamy, Bigoli with, *122–24*, *123*
Wine. *See* Prosecco

Y
Yogurt Cake, Fennel Seed and Candied-Peel, *50*, *51*

Z
Zabaione
   and Meringue Semifreddo, *268*, *269*
   Sauce, White Asparagus with, *108*, *109*
   Thick Hot Chocolate with, *62*, *63*
Zucchini
   Bacon, and Pecorino Tart, *100*, *101*
   Flowers, Ricotta and Mint–Stuffed, *88*, *89*
   Pecorino, and Fresh Mint Frittata, *184*, *185*
   Pizzette, *174*, *175*
   Shrimp, and Saffron, Tagliolini with, *125*, *126–27*